"What is it that makes freelancing so risky? In most cases it is not bad luck but bad planning that torpedoes the dream. That is why it is so important to take your business seriously right from the start. Your future is in your hands. Entirely.

"People who work nine-to-five jobs often wonder how I can write at home every day. My answer is very simple. I don't have a choice. It is what I love to do and what I have to do to survive. Necessity removes ambivalence."

The Freelancer's Business Book

Kalia Lulow

BALLANTINE BOOKS • NEW YORK

To T—
For gentle support
and tough advice

Library of Congress Catalog Card Number: 84-90861

ISBN 0-345-30355-5

Printed in Canada

First Edition: June 1984
Second Printing: December 1987

Table of Contents

Acknowledgments

I would like to thank Joëlle Delbourgo for her insight, support, and enthusiasm. Alice Fahs, my editor, deserves special recognition for her instincts and vision. Nancy Burke and Cynthia Katz provided valuable assistance in the preparation of the manuscript. And to my friends, who have been so steady as I rattle around in my footloose and freelance life—love.

1 Redefining Freelance

On the other side of the big plate glass window the sun cut through the narrow gap between the office buildings and lit the faces of passing pedestrians.

Sam stared down at them resentfully. "What do you do for a living?" he snarled. "How come you're out there and I'm stuck in here listening to Miss Crenshaw pop her gum and Old Man Winter complain about everything I do?"

Miss C. poked her head around his door. "Sam?" she said, between chews, "Better see the boss, pronto. There's trouble."

"There's gotta be a better way to earn a living," he muttered as he trudged to one more confrontation with his employer.

Ah! Freelance. What a life. No time clocks. No bosses. Strolls in the midday sun. Working when you like. Sleeping when you want. Selling your talents to the highest bidder. Doing what you do best.

It's Billy the Kid and Horatio Alger all rolled into one. The hired gun, the self-made millionaire: both are doers and dreamers. But just a moment!

Freelance work is much more and much less than that romanticized vision. Ask any freelancer and he or she will have a story to tell you—not just about the incredible rewards, but about the frustrations, too.

Jan D. started a shopping service when her second child entered school. She thought it would provide some income, but be flexible enough to allow her to run the house and care for her child.

"I didn't realize that even a part-time business required so much thought and planning. I didn't take care of the details of business for the first few months. I just got through each job and sighed with relief. All of a sudden I was buried under a mountain of untended paper work. I'm trying to catch up now. I hope to be able to get things under control soon, so I can make this work on a part-time basis."

Robert P., a very successful New York illustrator, works time and a half these days.

"I never knew work could be so much fun. It's all I ever wanted to do. I take it seriously and make sure it's rewarding, but nothing is more important to me than having a good time doing it."

No matter what type of freelancing you plan on doing, the one point to remember is that *all freelance means business*. Too long has it been seen as the namby-pamby land of late risers and cash-poor strugglers. Oh, you'll have good days and you'll have bad days. After all it's just like the rest of life. But when handled seriously, it can be the most rewarding and challenging type of work. This book helps you seize that opportunity.

The Business of Freelance

A freelance business is a special enterprise. It combines the pleasures and frustrations of self-employment with the courage and daring of the entrepreneurial spirit. Any successful freelancer is really a *freelance entrepreneur*.

Freelance means working on a job-by-job basis for a variety of clients. As a self-employed person, you do not earn your living on a regular salaried basis from any one source. Your employment depends on your talents and special skills. You must be able to sell yourself, to perform on demand, and to manage both the assignments that come your way and the business affairs that sustain your work.

Entrepreneurs are business people who have the bravery and aptitude for starting and running a business. They are a unique breed for, unlike conventional business persons, they find no comfort in the security of another's company...they want their own!

The blending of the freelance and entrepreneurial spirit offers the best chance for success in freelance business. The single-minded love of a job (almost always the mark of a self-employed person) combined with the adventuresome aptitude for business (that is at the heart of the entrepreneur) can form a solid basis for self-satisfaction and financial rewards.

Successful freelancers are special people. They are primarily motivated to start their own businesses because they can't work for anyone else. Their independent, free spirits make it difficult for them to follow others' directions. They want to be boss! Although they can manage a business, they have trouble delegating authority. Those who combine freelance work with full-time employment also possess these qualities. They are generally just in transition.

"I was never satisfied when I worked for a large accounting firm," recalls Fredrick G. "I didn't like having to deal with all the office politics and doing work according to a time clock instead of according to need." Now he's a freelance accountant with many different kinds of clients: small businesses and other self-employed people. "Some days I work eighteen hours, but some days I can take off and walk in the sun! I've got no one to answer to but myself. This is how I always dreamed life could be."

The difference between conventional entrepreneurs and freelance entrepreneurs is that freelancers do not think of themselves primarily as business people. Freelancers identify first with their talent or skill. The business is simply a device created to exercise that skill. Freelance businesses are idea businesses. They are developed by your looking into yourself and finding the activities that stimulate your imagination, motivate you, and call on your talents. The problems that most freelancers have stem from their reluctance to embrace the business side of their venture.

Jamie R., a successful magazine writer, adamantly declares, "I don't run a business. I hate business." Jamie's secret is that she is an unconscious entrepreneur. She would not be successful if she were really as out of touch with business as she claims. Upon careful questioning, she reveals that she does in fact keep tabs on her finances, make budgets, project income, set goals, and develop and maintain clients.

Many freelancers work as Jamie does. They do well because their talent is backed up by a natural business sense. But this can take them only so far. The key to growth and long-term stability is awareness of the business nature of their jobs. The key to self-satisfaction is a fanatic devotion to honing their talent. Redefining their work as a freelance entrepreneurship integrates these two basic qualities. It is an essential perspective. Freelance work—to be successful—must be approached as an entrepreneurial business, conducted as a business, controlled as a business.

Freelance Job Options

There are as many different kinds of freelancers as there are clever ideas. From part-timers to those who work around the clock, from artists to craftspersons, service people to household helpers, freelancers are involved in an enormous number of careers. As you begin to plan your enterprise, you need to know what options you have and to see what fits your time schedule, financial needs, and talents. Basically you can break the choices down into six categories:

Communications

This broad-based field covers everything from research to press agentry. It can involve writing, public relations, publicity, editorial services, secretarial and typing services, proofreading, and lecture services. Marion G.'s communications business, for example, specializes in artist relations. She helps musicians, theater people, and artists get the public notice they need in order to achieve and keep a good reputation. "I send out press releases, design openings, help put backers and artists together," Marion explains. Marion must be good at dealing with many kinds of personalities and she also needs writing, design, and production skills in her work.

Many of these freelance jobs can be developed from a current full-time occupation or can be begun slowly, job by job, until the freelancer amasses a track record. When full-time, such businesses are very demanding and require a flexible schedule and long hours. References and word-of-mouth recommendations are often the primary sources of new work.

Service

Service work covers an enormous range of duties, including: child care, cooking, housecleaning, shopping consultancy, personal organizing, travel planning, landscape and flower services, home repair, tutoring, interior design, and light moving.

Clarise W. started her plant services business after working for a florist for five years. Her clients include major corporations and individuals. "I have to give my clients what they want, even if they don't know anything about plants. They may leave the selection up to me, but I have to know the effect they are looking for. In addition, I have to maintain the plants I install—keep them healthy and beautiful," she explains.

Any work that is provided to a client to ease or improve his life in some way qualifies as a service. This category includes jobs that are well-suited to part-time or partial freelancing. Many do not call for special training, but simply an affinity or inherent talent.

Media

Media jobs include a whole roster of jobs in TV, radio, film, video, advertising, and audiovisual programming. They can be on either the technical or the creative side of the field. As a cameraman or sound engineer, you may find that your work involves dealing with unions or guilds. As a producer or director, the conceptualizing side of creating a product is emphasized. As a copywriter in advertising or as part of a production company, you are answering to many different masters.

Copywriter Joanne J. works full time for a national magazine, but always finds time to handle a variety of freelance clients as well.

"I can't take on anything that conflicts with my magazine's advertisers, but there is a whole world out there. Now I'm writing up a national campaign for a new at-home exercise gym. Launching a product is really exciting since you get to shape its image, not merely respond to an established one," Joanne notes.

Her skills have even taken her into ghost writing health and beauty books, since her ability to write zippy, direct prose translates well into nonfiction how-to style writing.

The media area is slightly different than the communications field, since so much of the work is done as an intensive team effort. This team quality can be an appealing break from the isolation of freelance work, but in some cases it makes the job more difficult and frustrating.

Business Consultancy

This is a high-level area that depends on expertise and connections in your area of specialization. Freelancers who are consultants generally have a work background in the field and a firm track record. Such areas as corporate communications, computer applications, marketing, and corporate promotion fall into this category too. Success here requires a tough business sense and the ability to work with corporate types.

Charles G. was an electrical engineer for ten years before he went out on his own as a consultant. "I have a wife and three kids, so it was very frightening to leave behind the security of a regular paycheck. But they have been very enthusiastic and helpful. My office is at home. When I meet clients it is usually at their offices or in a restaurant, so it has never been an inconvenience," Charles notes. "As a consultant, I get to keep expanding what I know, I'm not stuck in one small section of electrical engineering, repeating the same old tasks year after year. It's like being in school— and I love it," Charles observes. His clients must, too, since he is now earning three times as much as he did when he was a staff engineer.

Entertainment

From deliverers of singing telegrams to magicians, musicians, singers, actors, dancers, and disc jockeys, those who sell freelance entertainment often do so to generate an income while they pursue a professional career in the arts. They need a flexible business that uses their talents but doesn't keep them from being available when "legit" jobs come their way.

"Singing telegrams is not exactly the big time, but it pays the rent," explains Sally G. as she finishes putting on her top hat and tails to get ready for a night's work. "I trained to be an opera singer, but as you know that's a very tough field to make a living in. Your voice doesn't really mature 'til you're a lot older than I am. So I keep studying voice, going to auditions, and try to be optimistic about the future. In the meantime this is better for me than being a waitress."

Entertainers who have steady professional work in their field, well-employed artists and the like, are also freelancers. They need a business structure—often provided by business managers, agents, reps, and lawyers and accountants—to keep their work coming in.

Whichever category you fall into, you can have fun and make money doing what you love.

Visual Arts

The field of visual arts includes all crafts, illustration, graphic design, painting, book design, calligraphy, photography, and printing.

"The most fun I ever had with an assignment? I did a *Color Me Dog* coloring book for the National Canine Club, and a set of illustrations on body sounds for a book. But I also do more conventional commercial illustrations when I can get them. I'm not a great businesswoman, my drawings are very personal," Angie T. admits, "but I love my work. I mean really, getting paid to draw body sounds...what more could I ask for?"

Some of the visual arts fields are intensely personal and artistic, some more commercial and often done with or for a team. The competition is intense, as in any creative field, and both talent and business savvy must be keen to assure success.

How to Become a Freelance Entrepreneur

To create a successful freelance entrepreneurship, you need to follow five basic steps.

1. Find a business that uses your talents and skills.
2. Gear up your discipline and work habits for the stress of freelancing.
3. Set up a basic work environment so that you can get organized.
4. Evaluate your freelance business idea to see if it has the potential to be financially successful.
5. Learn how to sell yourself and work with your clients.

You are not ready to start a freelance business until you have gone through these five steps. You must prepare yourself for the rigors of running a business *and* performing your skill in a high-pressure environment.

Hard work and planning pave the way for good luck—something every freelancer needs! Luck is an elusive quality. Those who have it say it comes from hard work and a sharp eye for opportunity. Those without it resent its unfair distribution. But in truth it can come to anyone, and it's essential for freelance success. All it takes is relentless hard work, constant exposure to a wide variety of people and situations, and the ability to establish rapport and inspire confidence. You can achieve that if you dedicate yourself to successful freelance entrepreneurship.

So now that you're armed with the caution of the wisely scared and the bravery of the optimistic, it's time for you to begin your search for the freelance business that suits you.

2 Thinking It Over:
The Foundations of
Freelance Success

It's always 4 a.m. and raining when you finally admit something unpleasant is on your mind.

Sam swung his feet onto the cold, bare floor, turned on the bedside lamp, and reached for his cigarettes. "I gotta get out of that office," he muttered to Sarah, who lay dreaming of feline glory. "All you gotta do is eat and sleep. Wish I was a cat sometimes."

He cuffed her awake. "Well, what do you think? Can I do it? Can I go out on my own?"

Sam took her distracted scratching as agreement and, feeling much better, stubbed out the cigarette, turned out the light, and lay back.

There is good news and bad news. The good news is that anyone can start a freelance business. The bad news is that two-thirds of all such businesses fail within three years.

What is it that makes freelancing so risky? In most cases it is not bad luck but bad planning that torpedoes the dream. That is why it is so important to take your business seriously right from the start. Your future is in your hands—entirely.

In this chapter you have the chance to think it over

carefully. You want to develop a freelance business that is built on your strengths and skills and that suits your particular needs. To do this, you need to take the time to reflect on your business spirit (do you have the gumption to endure the stresses of freelancing?) and your abilities. You may have a vague feeling that you want to start a business but can't decide what type of enterprise is right for you. Or, you may know the field you want to enter but you may be unsure of how to focus it or how to judge your business acumen. Step by step you will uncover your potential and begin to formulate a concrete definition of your future entrepreneurship.

Step One: Assess Your Personality and Attitudes

The first step in deciding if you are a potential freelance entrepreneur is to assess your personality and attitudes as they relate to work. Good ideas are a dime a dozen. Talent is neither so rare nor so often rewarded that it assures success. The qualities that make a difference are those of approach and attitude.

"Something I've noticed in my classes on starting a business," reports attorney Fred I., whose practice includes small business management and law, "is that there is a definite entrepreneurial personality. Not brash or overly pushy. But quietly self-confident. Money does motivate, although for artists it is of secondary importance. But it seems like the attitude 'I'd rather do it myself' is the real key. A certain methodicalness, too. No inclination to make decisions from the seat of your pants. That's another factor. Solid financing helps. But nothing takes the place of hard work and confidence."

Before you even choose a freelance field, you must have discipline and motivation. Now these are qualities that we all want. But just telling you to have them is gratuitous. It's like saying, "be witty," or "be beautiful." You can't simply will them into existence. They must be cultivated, pursued, desired, for they are at the heart of the nature of the freelance beast.

Self-Discipline Is Vital

Few of us are as self-disciplined as we'd like to be. But you can nurture your self-discipline or kill it off, depending on your attitude toward your work. When you are ambivalent about what you have to do, it is a real battle to get work done. A freelancer must enjoy the work, find it fun. And he must be professional enough to do irksome and boring tasks that in the long run bring self-satisfaction and accomplishment. Starting a freelance business is a little like starting a football team all by yourself. You must be the offense and the defense, the coach and the water boy, the referee and the front office, the janitor and the superstar—and often even the fans. If you can't change hats, do the dirty work along with the glamor jobs, you will fail. A pro is someone who takes the bad without losing sight of the good. And a successful freelancer is a pro through and through.

When a job is difficult to get done, self-discipline is the only way through it. But if there is something inside you keeping you from being disciplined, ask yourself: "Am I afraid of success? Or failure? Do I feel so insecure that my self-esteem is eroded by doing less than the grandest tasks? Do I have long-range vision and goals?"

When I first started working as a freelance writer, I had to take on jobs that paid too little and were far too demanding. At least that's how they look in retrospect. But at the time I was so glad for the chance to be writing, so committed to doing a good job, that I worked on every project as though it were of earth-shaking importance. And to me they were. My self-discipline doesn't seem so amazing to me, but friends have always commented on it. I guess I just naturally knew that without it there would be no way to get ahead. It's a free commodity—no cost. And yet it almost guarantees results. It's one of the factors in freelancing that you really do have complete control over.

You will find that you have the stuff to tough it out when you don't indulge in self-pity or grandiose dreams. You have to crawl before you can walk and you have to earn your glory.

Self-discipline is a manifestation of a sense of purpose and enjoyment. If you cultivate those two qualities, you will find that discipline follows naturally. Don't impose discipline arbitrarily from the outside. You'll just rebel; it's human nature. Make it part and parcel of your process of striving for freelance success.

Motivation—Another Vital Quality

You have got to have the drive to work very hard. There are an infinite number of reasons for personal motivation. They can run the gamut from the desire to make money, to the desire to prove to your parents that you're talented, to the wish to see your name in lights. These are the primal sources of motivation. Desire to pay the rent or eat dinner are more superficial prods, but should not be ignored. Necessity is a great motivator.

People who work 9-to-5 jobs often wonder how I can write at home every day. My answer is very simple. I don't have a choice. It is what I love to do and what I have to do to survive. Necessity removes ambivalence.

You can foster motivation by combining the feeling of necessity with the desire to reach your dreams and goals. Remember, few things feel as good as a sense of achievement.

Ambition—The Silent Fire

Ambition, like aggression, has a bad name to some people. It connotes the kind of ruthless self-centered push for the top that many "creative" people disavow. But ambition is really a simple, pure feeling that comes from the desire to be rewarded for one's skills. And when used correctly, it makes you work very hard to hone your skills so that they are top quality. Freelance work is fiercely competitive. Without ambition, a free-lancer is condemned to flounder every time he comes up against competition for work. So admit to the silent fire—burning ambition—and use it to make yourself work hard and long and well. It gives a sense of purpose to the arduous tasks you face.

Flexibility and Resourcefulness

Flexibility and resourcefulness are two other key qual-ities shared by all successful freelance entrepreneurs. Just because you plan and organize your own business does not mean the world will fall in line behind you. When you are dealing with a variety of clients, you are going to encounter a lot of unexpected problems, demands, desires, and perspectives. Whether it is in negotiating, setting fees, delivering completed work, or handling finances, each situation will present some new twist—usually when you least expect it.

Your work schedule may fail, your patience dete-riorate, but you can't let that throw you. Freelance work is rather like cooking without following a recipe. You must learn what substitutions can be made in the ingredients without jeopardizing the end result. A sense of feel, a visceral tuned-in-ness to what's going on around you must be developed.

"I thought I was hired to cater a wedding. Little did I know the family would expect me to select invita-tions, arrange flowers, and contract the music, too." Frank N. still shakes his head when he remembers one of his first catering jobs, four years ago. "I wasn't ready to take on the kind of full-service work that my client expected. Not that they had told me ahead of time that they expected it! I could have refused, but I think I would have lost the job altogether if I had. And besides, I needed the work."

Frank's story is a classic case of having to be in-stantly flexible—which of course means "instantly resourceful." Frank found sources for advice and hired other freelancers to help him with the flowers. He found a way to fill his client's demands. It took a toll on him in terms of time and stress, but his client never knew. As for adjusting the contract so that he was paid fairly for the extra work—well, that could have gone better. "But I got another job, through one of the guests at the wedding, so I guess the investment paid off!" Frank concludes.

Self-Confidence

Everyone wants to be coolly confident. But it's a rare quality, and if it were necessary for success, there would be more failures than there are. However, uncool self-confidence is a valuable and necessary quality.

Lynn D. is the founder and head of Innovative Information Techniques, a corporate communications consultancy. When she started, under very adverse conditions, she had no job, no office, and no clients. Her fifteen years as a college teacher made her either overqualified or underqualified for every one of the 85, yes 85, job interviews she went to. But she dug in, decided to start her own business, and depended on her "survival mentality."

"I refused to fail. I worked eighteen hours a day, seven days a week. And I was scared. But at the same time I knew I could do things before I'd done them for the first time. I was in a panic but also confident.

"I don't think I'll ever get over being nervous and scared. I still get absolutely crazy, as I did when I didn't know if I'd be able to pay the rent. I've learned, however, to avoid projecting the 'scareds.' My clients have always thought I had a big organization behind me. But 'til a year ago there was no one but me doing it all. And I admit I still poke my nose in everything. I guess I made my nervousness work for me so my confidence could grow alongside it. The two now coexist pretty peacefully."

Confidence is part determination, part faith, and part

the result of accomplishment. Nurture it. Feed it. Act on it.

Step Two: Identify Your Abilities

Are you undaunted? Does the challenge of using your best personal qualities and developing them further make you eager to get your business started? If so, you're a good candidate for freelance work.

To find a business that will succeed, you must select a field that you enjoy and in which you are skilled. It is surprising how out of touch with our skills we can be. We take for granted that other people can do what we can, but this is not the case. You need to identify your abilities; from these, you'll generate business ideas.

You need to answer three basic questions about yourself.

1. What are my skills and talents that I could use as a basis for a business?
2. How do I manage my current business affairs?
3. Do I seem to have the ability to manage a business venture?

The answers to these questions may not pop immediately into your mind. So take the time to examine your past work experience, talents, and managerial skills by writing out a detailed history of each.

Generate a Job-Experience List

This process is much like writing a mega-resume. You need to become aware of your skills and then sell them, first to yourself and then to the world.

Begin by writing a list of all the jobs you've ever had, from paper boy to baby-sitter, secretary to waitress; no job is too insignificant. Include full-time jobs, summer jobs, part-time ones, and volunteer work, too.

List the duties and work you performed under each job title. Include minor and incidental tasks as well as general job descriptions. For example, if you were a salesperson, you had to handle money, take care of stock, deal with accounting procedures, perhaps work a computerized register, have good rapport with the public, practice salesmanship, learn your line of merchandise, and often act as a shopping or gift-purchasing advisor.

As a file clerk, you may have done general organizational work, phone work, typing, dealt with complicated procedural systems, and been a diplomat, to boot.

Think about what you did in each job that made you mutter, "Boy, are they lucky to have me around!" Those extra efforts, that ability to assume responsibility and cover extra bases, probably expanded the skills you used or developed.

If I were to generate a job-experience list of work I had before I went freelance, it would look like this:

Waitress

–served food—both fast and elegant French service
–learned about wines
–managed money
–handled bills and occasionally did cashier work
–developed good ability to deal with the public
–developed time-management and organizational skills
–used memory and concentration
–learned to work under high pressure

Assistant, Rare Books Room, University of Wisconsin Library

–learned about microfilm
–learned about library systems and procedures
–gained information on rare book titles
–expanded ability to deal with the public
–expanded organizational skills

Substitute Teacher

–learned about planning lessons and organizing a class
–learned to dodge spit balls
–learned to teach Spanish when I don't know a word of it
–learned child psychology
–expanded ability to deal with ever-changing high-pressure situations
–expanded ability to handle the demands of many people (not quite "the public") with diplomacy and fast thinking

Social Secretary to Contessa Christina Paolozzi Bellin

–further expanded organizational skills—party and travel planning and scheduling particularly
–handled correspondence
–further expanded ability to deal with a wide variety of people
–baby-sitter and dog-walker!

Publishing Manager, Delegates World Bulletin

–learned reporting, writing, editing skills on bi-monthly UN newspaper
–learned to conduct interviews
–learned about print production, layout, and making mechanicals
–further expanded organizational skills
–further expanded ability to deal with the public
–further developed ability to work under pressure

Assistant Production Manager, Civil Engineering Magazine

–learned about advertising business
–learned layout of four-color magazine
–expanded knowledge of production
–expanded proofreading skills
–expanded ability to do correspondence
–learned office organization and expanded organizational skills

Well, that's my job experience up to the time I went freelance seven years ago. What did it prepare me for, you ask? Serving food to UN delegates? Handling the social affairs of magazine editors who read rare books? Those don't sound like very promising business ideas!

What I can identify is the ability to handle a wide variety of situations; good rapport with people; an interest in learning new jobs; and an accumulation of confidence that comes with getting out into the world and coping. Your job list may be much more orderly. Your training and experience may lead you into one or two clearly defined areas of expertise. But if they don't, don't despair. You have (as I did) another chance...your skills list.

Generate a Skills List

We all have skills that we do not use in our jobs. They are for our own pleasure or self-maintenance. These too can provide a basis for a freelance business. As a matter of fact, if you are like me and do not have a conventional job-experience list to use as a basis for your future freelance business, a skills list is your best resource. You don't need advanced degrees to start a business. You need advanced abilities. So this is your chance to blow your own horn. Don't be shy.

List all your talents, hobbies, and skills. Cooking, child care, needlework, other crafts, yard work, house plantings, household organization, furniture repair or refinishing, writing, photography, shopping...there is no item too "ordinary.") What we take for granted, others often cannot or will not do for themselves. Arrange this list in order of proficiency. Then identify those abilities that bring you the most pleasure.

Pinpoint the three activities that inspire you most. Don't choose one over the other. Mull them over; examine the potential of each.

Assess Your Business Savvy

A freelance business is just that—a business. You must be skilled at the job *and* capable of managing the machinery that keeps the work coming. Some freelance enterprises demand more business ability than others, so you want to choose one that you can handle. You don't have to have an MBA to be competent at complex business matters, but you do need to have a basic aptitude and an interest in business matters. How you handle your personal business affairs can give you a clue to how you'd handle your business. So be honest and objective.

Evaluate how you manage your money. Do you keep good records? Do you file your taxes on time? Do you plan a personal budget? Stick to it? Do you save money? Is your checkbook a mess?

Now, all of us mess up on a couple of those counts. That doesn't mean we can't run our own businesses. But this evaluation does tell us where we will continue to mess up. Then the choice is yours: to improve or continue tormenting yourself. If you are truly incompetent, or rate yourself deficient on most of the questions, you should try to uncover the source of your business reluctance. Handling business is really just taking care of yourself well. Neglecting it to the point of trouble is self-destructive behavior.

Ask four freelancers how they manage money and chances are you'll get four tales of woe.

"Money? If I never had to think about it, I would work better."

"Frankly, I never could keep track of all my receipts and records. I just gave up. I pile everything into an envelope and dump it on my accountant's desk four times a year."

"When I was broke all the time, I was terrible. But now that it's not so depressing, I do better with money management."

"It's one more year that I've screwed up my taxes. Don't ask! I don't know why I can't get on top of it."

Whether you are successful or not, money is the universal hassle of the self-employed. Why not try to spare yourself the stress and start now, in the very beginning, to take charge of it?

Look at your business experience. Have you ever been in a job that required you to handle money? Balance budgets? Keep books? Did you enjoy it, or hate it? Did you perform well?

Think about how you handle job interviews. Are you confident, comfortable? Do you manage your nervousness? Can you sell yourself? Most freelance jobs require a lot of self-selling! If you seriously doubt your ability to become more comfortable with job-interview situations, then perhaps you need a more steady job (or a business partner).

Reflect on your general comfort level with business people. Do suits and ties make you see red? Are you disdainful of "corporate types"? Does a plush office make you nostalgic for the Yippies? If so, you are going to have to find a job that doesn't thrust you into such situations. AND you're going to have to tone down your reactions. I know this is a touchy subject. We covet our "otherness," we freelance types. But you want to do what you want to do—and do it well, for as much money as possible. So what's the percentage if you get in your own way with a bunch of belligerent attitudes?

Step Three: Choose a Business

Now it's time to use the information that you've collected about yourself to come to a decision about the type of freelance entrepreneurship you want to start. To do this, you need to consider how much time you can devote to the business, engage your inspiration, and then look at your specific qualifications as they apply to your business ideas.

Rate Your Freelance IQ

How high is your Freelance Inspiration Quotient? It's time to test it—to see what inspired ideas you can come up with. Remember, the secret to true inspiration is that it delights as a fantasy and is possible as a reality!

1. Read over your job-experience list and your skills list. What stands out as your area of expertise? What auxiliary talents, such as general organizational skills, knowledge of food service, familiarity with business procedures, stand out?
2. Pick three general business areas that appeal to you.
3. Under each, write as many qualifying specifics as you can, so that you begin to define the possible scope of the ideas. For example: if cooking appeals to you, answer the following questions:

   –Will it be a catering service, or sales to retail outlets of your product?

   – If it is catering, will it be for individual parties or for business clients?

   –What type of food or cuisine will you prepare? Will you make one or two specialties or a vast menu?

4. Mull each idea over. Don't jump to conclusions yet. Let the ideas percolate. Play with them. Imagine yourself actually working at the jobs for a living.

Assemble Your Credentials

Now it's time to examine your credentials in each of the three possible business areas. This is truly resumé-writing, and is unlike the general job- and skill-evaluation in that here you want to narrow your credentials list to the specific tasks involved in each idea.

1. Write out your demonstrated track record in each area.

2. List your proven skills if you have no track record.

3. Imagine that potential clients are going to be "sold" on you by your credentials. Do they sound convincing?

4. Consider how you can present yourself to clients. If you have a track record, are references available? Does your job history alone impress? If you are selling a service such as house painting, landscaping, furniture refinishing, do you have photographs of your work to show what you can do? If you are a designer, photographer, or craftsperson, do you have a portfolio? As a publicist, writer, PR or publicity person, do you have samples? If you lack tangible "evidence," can you assemble it or make samples that are of professional quality?

5. Review your three "resumes." Which is strongest? Can you find ways to enhance the others? Which one makes you most excited about the realistic possibilities of getting freelance work?

You should be narrowing the field by now, but there's one more consideration before you finalize your decision.

Make a Time Commitment

Freelancing can be very time-consuming. But if you choose well and plan carefully, it can work out on a part-time basis. Your choice must take into consideration how much time you can or want to devote to it *and* how much time the business itself requires to be done well. Some fields demand that you work full time to maintain your credibility.

1. Decide just how much time you have. Do you have to juggle child care, school, full-time job, or family obligations? Your schedule may permit freelancing only on weekends or evenings.

2. Be realistic about how much energy and time you have. Don't plan on overextending yourself!

Tim W., a Nashville photographer, kept his teaching job for several years before he went full-time freelance. He notes, "For a long time I floundered around. I'd start a project but never do it as well as I'd like because I was always running out of time. In the beginning I just wasn't organized enough to do both [freelance and teaching]. Eventually I learned how to do it. That made things go so well that I moved to full-time photography." Tim learned that even part time must be approached seriously. "In the beginning I was dreaming more than scheming," he concludes.

3. Ask yourself, "How much money do I hope to make from this?" You will have a chance to do a detailed financial plan for your business in Chapter Three and Six, but for now, simply try to determine if the amount of time that you can commit will, realistically, generate the earnings you want.

4. Decide if you are a candidate for full-time or part-time freelancing.

5. Decide if any or all of your business ideas will work within the time you have available.

Make a Choice

The time has come, the walrus said, to speak of just one thing. What will it be? As you've gone through the above steps you (probably) have felt that one idea is more exciting, more viable, or more realistic than the others. So act on your feelings and thoughts. Take a stand, make a decision.

Live with it. Let it float around in your imagination. Ask your friends about it. Talk to other freelancers in the field.

Let your enthusiasm build. Then you'll be ready to go through the detailed work of examining your idea's true business potential.

3 The Preliminary Business Plan

For the fourth time in as many days Sam bolted out of his office and started down the hall to Ol' Man Winter's office.

"I'm cashing it in."

"Well, this is it, chief."

"So long, sucker!"

But none of the phrases had the ring he was looking for.

Sam stopped. Again. "When am I going to get outta here?" he cried to no one in particular. "I need a plan."

Disgusted with himself, he turned on Miss Crenshaw. "I'm going to lunch," he yelled.

"But it's only 10 o'clock," she sputtered as he marched down the back stairs in search of the nearest bar.

You know you want to start a freelance business.

The sense of urgency is building.

You can't wait to get the first job.

But not so fast!

Before you charge off pell-mell, full of fight and fire, you need to investigate the real pros and cons of your entrepreneurial idea. Businesses cannot be run on dreams. This isn't a Tinkerbell world where wishing makes things real. Dreams and wishes are essential motivating forces. They inspire. They make hard work and struggle seem meaningful. But they don't prepare you for the day-to-day battle with the real world.

A Preliminary Business Plan (PBP) is a way of measuring your dreams and wishes against reality. It lets you examine the feasibility of your idea—in ten steps you'll uncover its strengths and weaknesses. You'll hone the definition of your business, find out what it will take to make money and if you can afford the risks.

To launch any business you must be able to answer four basic questions:

1. Is there a reasonable market or need for my business product or service?
2. Can I afford to underwrite the start-up of my business?
3. Can I generate and maintain clients?
4. Can I make a profit?

The PBP gives you answers to these questions. But the process of preparing the plan is difficult. It requires discipline. It doesn't assure success, but it does help guard against failure. If you do a thorough plan, you will have demonstrated that you have the gumption to do the hard work of actually running a business. If you can't get through the assignments in this chapter, you might as well forget the whole venture. You are just too lazy, too much of a dreamer—not enough of a doer!

A Look at the Other Side of the Coin

Now after all that highfalutin' talk and harsh language, I do have to admit that there is another perspective...one that bears consideration.

It's the jump-off-the-diving-board-without-looking-to-see-if-the-pool's-got-any-water-in-it technique. But you aren't going to catch me advocating it!

True, I'm advocating that you do as I say and not as I did. But then, you get the benefit of my hindsight!

For when I went freelance seven years ago, I didn't have the slightest idea of whether or not I'd be able to pay next month's rent. I quit my 9-to-5 and never looked back. I didn't feel I had any choice. I'd always wanted to be a writer, and I'd reached a point where it seemed to me that I'd either have to be brave enough to try *right then* or admit that I didn't have what it takes, *ever*.

Looking back, I can say that it worked out just fine. But there were months, totaling years, when I worked fourteen hours a day and barely made enough money to eat. I was carried along by the sheer joy of writing, but the thrill I felt to be doing what I'd always dreamed of, no matter what the price. I learned to handle the business slowly. My first task was to be writing all the time, and to have no alternative, but keep at it. If I'd had a backup job, some easy way out, I might never have gone through my grueling apprenticeship.

So, I'm like an anxious parent, hoping to be able to spare you some of the unnecessary pain I went through. But I don't want to protect you from life too much, either. You have to make mistakes to learn how to think on your feet and cope.

So, bearing all this seemingly contradictory information in mind, it's time to try to strike a balance between the impulsive dream of freelance and its all too real demands. Settle down with a pencil and a cup of coffee and read through the following plan. Then go back to the first step and begin the process of evaluation and preparation for your entrance into the business world.

Step One: Define Your Business

What *are* you going to be doing?

The answer seems so obvious that you probably haven't put much thought into it. When your friends ask, "What exactly is this business idea?," you answer,

"Oh, you know. I'll be consulting companies on their corporate communications systems." Or, "I'll offer businesses complete plant and flower-arrangement services." Or, "I'm going to do catering, cooking for parties and stuff." But exactly what does *consulting* mean to you? What businesses are you providing plant services to and what does "complete" mean? Whom are you going to cook for? What kinds of parties do you want to cater and what types can you handle? Unless these types of particular questions are answered in your business definition, you don't really know what you want to do, or what you can do.

So try to give as well-thought-out a definition as is possible at this point. As you go through the rest of this plan, you will become aware of all the details that go into creating a proper business definition. When you are through with the plan, you'll see how much more targeted your definition becomes!

Step Two: Investigate Rules and Regulations

Many businesses, regardless of size, are regulated by state or federal agencies. Food services, schools of all kinds, employment agencies, child care facilities, and many others must meet certain minimum health and safety standards. As a rule of thumb, any business that serves the public may fall into this category. However, state to state there is no uniform code; I suggest that you check with your State Department of Commerce or ask a lawyer if your business needs licensing or authorization of some kind. The cost of a license must be figured into your budget.

"I run this nursery school because it's what I know how to do and what I enjoy," explains Nina R. over the voices of ten 3-year-olds who are playing in her living room.

"Some mothers, well, they go out of the home to work, and that gives me a job. But I could never do that. I'd miss my kids if they spent the day with some-one else," Nina observes.

Nina (not her real name) runs one of the thousands of private day care centers that have sprung up all over the country to answer the changing needs of the American family.

"I know some places have all kinds of stuff, thousands of dollars of toys and games. But my kids here, they have each other. They like to use their imaginations. There is a nice yard. We all have fun. I do think they get smarter—smarter about being with other people. And themselves."

Does Nina worry that she doesn't have state certification? No, she feels her setup is casual enough to avoid detection. All business comes from references and word of mouth. She is running a risk, though, for she could be forced out of business.

That happened to Kathy. She started a typing instruction business in her home. With local advertising, she grew and grew until she had two classes running every month. But then some state official came to inspect the premises. It did not meet the exacting standards for a commercial school: for it was, after all, only her home. The result? Business shut down. Kathy chose not to find a commercial space and really take the leap into running a full-fledged school. Her freelance dreams ended and she went back to being an executive secretary for a large company.

Don't think just because you are small you will escape notice. Too many freelance businesses have been closed down because they failed to follow proper procedures.

Step Three: Evaluate Start-Up Costs

Can you afford to start your business? Everything from paper clips to word processors, light bulbs to business cards, must be considered. Freelancers face a dilemma. They want to assemble the symbols of business in order to establish external reality—if your stationery says you're a business then you must be—but they don't really know how to determine what items they *must* have to succeed and what items they simply *want*, to make themselves feel better. Freelancers often either rush out and spend a fortune on unnecessary gizmos or end up undersupplied and limp along foolishly. To avoid either extreme, you should come up with a list of those supplies and equipment that you *must* have to get going. You can then augment that with a second list of necessary but not primary needs. Once you see how much these items will cost and compare it to the amount of cash you have available, you will know if you've got a reasonable or unrealistic idea.

To fill out the Start-Up Costs Table on page 31, use the listing here as a start-off point. You may need special equipment, or perhaps you already have ample supplies of some. You may have to create an office from scratch, or perhaps you already have a "den" that you can easily convert. If you are starting a catering service, for example, you may eventually need ten cake pans of various sizes and shapes. But in the beginning four will let you be sufficiently prepared for work. Buy additional ones as the need arises. This principal applies to all businesses.

Once you have identified what you need to get started, go shopping and compare prices. Find the best deals. Then separate items into "rock-bottom basics" and "beyond basics." From these two lists you'll get a solid idea of the amount of money you must spend.

Step Four: The Cost of Living

You have to be able to eat and sleep while you launch your business—or at least have the possibility available! What is your personal monthly budget? How much money do you have to earn to sustain your life—and to meet your responsibilities to family and children, if

Start-Up Costs Table

	Rock-Bottom Basics		Beyond Basics	
Office Supplies	Description	Cost	Description	Cost
stationery				
typewriter				
answering machine				
pens, paper, etc.				
Phone Service				
new line				
answering service				
answering machine				
Office Furniture				
desk				
chair				
lamp				
file cabinets				
Specialized Equipment				
the tools of your trade				
Preliminary Advertising				
flyers				
brochures				
print ads				
Office Space				
(only if absolutely necessary for running your business!)				
	Total: ___		Total: ___	

you have any? How are you going to meet these obligations while getting your business started: by keeping your current 9-to-5 job? by living off savings? by depending on income generated from your freelance business?

To figure this out, you must know what you need each month. Go back over your checkbook stubs for

the last year. See what kinds of expenses you incurred.
Then generate a realistic budget.

ROCK BOTTOM MONTHLY COSTS:	BEYOND BASICS MONTHLY COSTS:
Rent/Mortgage_____	Entertainment_____
Food_____	Travel_____
Phone_____	Clothing_____
Utilities_____	Other_____ (If you have kids, this is no small category!)
Insurance_____ (If payments are quarterly, figure annual fee and divide by 12 for monthly expense.)	
Transportation_____ (For car, count gas, upkeep, insurance, parking.)	
$_____ (Total Cost)	$_____ (Total Cost)

Step Five: A Margin of Safety

To launch a business, you must have a reasonable
margin of safety. What is "reasonable"? What is
"safety"? There are no set answers to these questions,
but you can determine what will work for you personally. Your assessment must be based on: (1) your responsibilities; (2) your living expenses; (3) your cash
reserves; (4) your ability to earn money immediately;
(5) your hysteria/panic level.

Your Responsibilities

If it's just you and the landlord, you don't have to worry about anyone's welfare but your own. Remember, when you are self-employed you must buy your own health insurance. Don't neglect this. If you can't afford it, you can't afford to start a business. One minor accident or illness could wipe you out! In other ways, however, you may be able to afford to take chances. How well-suited you are to risk-taking has to do with your hysteria/panic level. (More about that later.) If, however, you must support or contribute to the support of a family, you cannot afford to risk failure as easily as can a person with fewer responsibilities.

Your Living Expenses

Based on your monthly budget, you know how much money you need to survive. If it is a lot, then you must be able to make your business work quickly and have some kind of fallback position if it doesn't bring in money quickly enough.

Your Cash Reserves

This brings us naturally to your cash reserves. If you have a lot of responsibilities or expenses, then you must be able to meet them through a salaried job, savings, a rich uncle, or some other means that doesn't make it absolutely mandatory that your business hit the Fortune 500 within a month. How much reserve do you have? How many months can it cover if you have no other money coming in?

Your Ability to Earn Money Immediately

If you are going freelance with one or two solid clients in your pocket, you can count on some income for some length of time. I say "some" because in the free-lance life a job in the hand is worth...well, on a bad day, almost nothing. Jobs can change, disappear, or simply not repeat; and what you've counted on may not in fact materialize. So project your income only when you are really, really sure that it will in fact come through.

Your Hysteria/Panic Level

Nerves of steel or mush? Do you get scared when you get broke, or do you get going? Are you depressed or challenged by adversity? Only you know the answers to these questions. But they must be answered, for if you plan to go freelance, the viability of your idea depends on your stamina. The same idea might be good for one person and bad for another. If you need a year's security to move into full-time freelance and you only have three month's worth—then you are going to be very unhappy. But if you can wing it on a three-month cushion and not panic, then...hey, full time here you come! For some, part-time freelancing may be the best. Keeping your full-time job while you launch the business does provide financial security.

So reflect. *Think about it*. Then ask yourself: "How many months' cushion do I need?"

Remember, your initial costs include:

1. Monthly living expenses
2. Business start-up costs.

Once you have thought about these important is-sues, you will have determined how many months you are going to give yourself to actually get the business running—that is, earning money. There is no set an-swer, but a 4- to 6-month cushion seems comfortable for many people. One hint: it costs money to keep it going! New supplies, additional advertising, extra equipment will all be necessary during this start-up phase. You must be able to meet those needs as they arise, too!

Step Six: Researching the Market

When you are just starting a business, it seems that a lot of people must need your service. But in truth, it is a specific group of as yet unknown people who will provide you with your bread-and-butter business. You want to hone in on them as soon as possible. See what it is that *you* offer that makes you distinct from others working in your same general field. Determine *who* can use your special talents. Find out exactly who your competition is. Learn about their rates, standards, level of quality and service. Find ways of positioning your business so that it offers something extra. You cannot be all things to all clients. You can't be discount and deluxe, personalized and high volume. It is important to see what is needed in your area and what suits you. This is a vital step in clarifying your business definition. Without it, you will spread yourself too thin and waste time and money trying to secure unlikely or inappropriate clients.

Your goal is to generate a list of specific services, skills, or products that you will offer. To help you do this, follow the steps below:

Investigate the Competition

If there is none, ask yourself: Is this because no one has been clever enough to think of this yet, *or* because it is not a viable business in this locale?

If there is some competition, check through local papers and the telephone book to find out the names

and locations of competitors. Contact them. Ask about
rates and services. No need to say you are a potential
rival; you are simply shopping. Go look at their setup if this will help you plan your business.

If you are going into a business that does not advertise, such as writing, your best bet is to ask friends
and friends of friends if they know anyone in your field.
Make arrangements to go to talk to these people.
Chances are they will gladly give you any information
you need.

Check Reference Sources for Information

Check reference sources for information about trade
associations, unions, guilds, and other organizations
that are concerned with your business. Check *The Encyclopedia of Organizations*, published by Gale Research, for a list of all such groups. (See Chapter 10
for more specific information.) Such groups usually
have a wealth of information about how to run the
business, rate standards, and general organizational
guidelines. This information is invaluable.

List Potential Clients

Make a list of potential clients. Keep it general at first.
If you are a graphic artist who does mechanicals, you
might list restaurants, retail stores, local newspapers,
or people who publish broadsheets as potential clients.
Look in papers and magazines to see if your potential
clients already advertise. Do you think you could design better ads? Provide more effective layout? Begin
to list potential clients. If you will provide a service to
individuals instead of to other businesses, you must
sleuth out clients and figure out how to get their attention. For example, if you are going to run a typing
service, ask yourself, "Where do people who need typists work or do business?" Many students need typists,
so posting notices at schools or handing out flyers on

college campuses might put you in touch with potential clients. If you are going to run a day care center, notices in grocery stores or church bulletins are effective, as are flyers at playgrounds. For any service to individuals, ads in neighborhood papers are also effective.

List The Services or Products You Offer

Is it complete? Too large? What is your specialty? What makes you distinctive? Review the list. Spend time getting it concise and accurate. Write it out! This is now the heart of your business definition, and from it all your sales pitches, rate scales, and public relations image decisions will flow. You need the core of your business to be expressed clearly and precisely whenever you talk to anyone about what you do.

Step Seven: Setting Rates

Once you know exactly how much money you have to earn and what kinds of goods or services—exactly—you will offer, it is time to try to determine how much you will charge. Your fees must be in line with local standards so that you will be competitive. They must be consistent. They must provide you with a living wage.

Setting rates is tricky. You might discover that the local rate for typing is $1.25 a page. If you need $1,500.00 a month, that means you'll have to type 1,200 pages a month to make a living! Well, that comes to many pages, and many clients on a very steady basis. If you can't charge more—say, $2.00 a page—and remain competitive, then you're not going to succeed with this freelance business!

Setting rates is a crucial step in determining the viability of your business idea. There are two basic types of rates: fee-for-service with expenses not included and set rates with expenses included.

Generally, each business field has its own traditional approach. But you might consider the following pros and cons to each method of fee-setting.

Fee-for-service charges the client on a per job, daily, or hourly rate for time and then adds expenses on top of that. Photographers often bill in this way. They may charge a fee of $500 per day *plus* expenses. The fee-for-service rate tells the client exactly how much you personally are making. Since the client knows the expenses are set, the client may try to lessen the overall cost by chiseling your fee down. However, the advantage is that you are never going to find yourself in the position of having so badly underestimated your expenses that you end up losing all your income to cover your expenses, because the two don't come out of the same pot. You will, however, be responsible for providing an accurate estimate of potential expenses. You can't afford to be far off the mark, so add a 10% surcharge to protect yourself. And don't tell your client you've done so!

Set rates include everything—your time, costs, and expenses. You give your customer one inclusive cost, not broken down. The set rate method is high-risk. You *must* correctly estimate your expenses before you incur them. If you are wrong, it's money out of your pocket. For examples, if you are a house-painter and charge a set fee per room, say, $200, that is all you have to cover costs *and* make a profit. However, if you overestimate, add a 10% surcharge on some items, and get some lucky breaks, you can end up making more money than you originally predicted. It can cut either way.

In either case, fee-for-service or set rate, you must always know how much it will cost you to do a job and how much you must make above costs. To determine this you must research job-related expenses carefully. Try to develop relationships with your suppliers so that you can get quality at low cost.

Figuring out how much you must make on any job is more difficult than estimating costs. You are restricted by the going rates in your field and by the fact that you are new and don't necessarily have the reputation to charge premium fees yet. You probably won't really know how much time you will have to put in on any job in the beginning. Chances are you'll put in more time than needed, just because you're not really operating at peak efficiency. The rules of thumb, however, are:

1. Estimate the time involved to complete the job.
2. Figure out what percent of your available monthly time you need to spend to complete the job.
3. Calculate what percent of your monthly required income must be earned in this length of time. Voila! Your basic rate. Anything beyond that is cause for joy.

Let's look at an example.

You are going to do a landscaping job. You will bill fees separate from expenses. You estimate that the job will take four days.

Every month you must earn $1,000. Four days is one-fifth of your working time available in a month. Therefore, you must clear $200 profit in those four days.

But $200 is far too small a fee for the job. And chances are you won't have 20 days' worth of work in a month. You know the going rate for landscapers in your area is $15 an hour. Four 8-hour days can be billed at $480.00. Hey! This is a business that might just work! If you can get five more days of work this month, you'll get by!

On the other hand, let's look at the typing service again. You need $1,500 a month. You can type 40 pages a day without losing your mind. You have a 200-page manuscript to type. It will take you 5 to 6 days. If you charge $2.00 a page, you'll earn $400 in 5 days. You will have to type 40 pages a day for 18 days—or 720 pages—to make $1,440 a month. And you'll be blind and completely exhausted by the end of your first month! To augment your income without increasing your typing load consider offering auxillary services such as editing, proofreading or rewriting.

Whatever your business, figure out the minimum amount of work you *must* do to get by and the maximum amount you *can* do, and see if you can get paid a living wage for it.

Step Eight: Generating Clients

The rates are set, the market researched; now it's time to make a preliminary investigation to see if you can actually secure paying customers.

In Chapter 4 you will learn in more detail how to sell yourself and your new business by writing a proposal, brochures, and promotional literature. For now, you are simply testing the waters to prepare yourself *if* and *when* you decide you are actually going to launch this business.

Running a freelance business is like being trapped in a continual job interview, since you must constantly generate new clients. This is the most difficult and most important part of running your business. Confidence and success at securing clients come only with practice; I suggest that you begin to polish your technique by targeting four potential customers. Choose them wisely; they should be realistic possibilities. If you are going into the entertainment field and hope to do a magic act at kids' parties, start with people you know— or who can refer you to potential clients. Don't start by trying to interest people who don't know you and to whom you have no introduction. If you are going to do window displays for shops, don't try to get Saks to hire you! Go for the small local boutique or gift store, the family-run stationery store down the street, or the local hardware store, where you are known.

Once you have chosen four potential clients, write, call, or go talk to them about your service. If you write to them, keep the letter simple and clear.

- State the name of your business.
- Explain why you have chosen to write to them.
- List the services you offer.

After the initial contact, arrange a meeting so that you can discuss your service and begin to find out what your potential clients are looking for and need. Their input will tell you what you have overlooked in your business definition. You may find out that you need to offer pickup and delivery to your typing clients, or that you will have to provide a catering connection or party favors along with performing your magic act at children's parties. You may not have realized the kind of auxiliary services that clients desire and that, when offered, make you a more appealing choice than your competition.

If in this process of contact and conversation you actually secure a client—go for it! Take the job. Try your idea out in the real world. You will gather valuable information and discover untold things about what it will feel like to actually jump into the business when the time comes to make your move.

Step Nine: Projecting Income and Expenses

Alas, you cannot know what you will earn in your freelance business before you earn it. But you can make some kind of projection that takes into account definite and potential income, at least during the first three-month period after you officially begin working.

To do this, you must create a balance sheet that adds up all your definite contracted income for jobs you have lined up already *and* realistically takes into account those jobs that seem to be in the offing in the next few months. From that figure you must subtract your business and personal expenses over the same time period. The resulting figure will tell you if you can make it or not—*maybe*. Since the income projection may not be firm, there is an element of chance. You can minimize but not eliminate it, since freelance is a chancy life.

Income and Expenses Balance Sheet—Three-Month Projection

Income: Contracted (estimate of amount earned): _____
           Possible (estimate of amount earned): _____
           a. Total estimated income for 3-months: _____

Expenses: Personal expenses estimate for three months: _____
           b. Business expenses, 3-month estimate
             Rent: _____
             Office supplies: _____
             Postage: _____
             Advertising: _____
             Business entertaining: _____
             Office help: _____
             Accountant and lawyer fees: _____
             Miscellaneous: _____
           c. Total estimated cost of maintaining business
             for three months: _____
           Balance (sum of b&c subtracted from a): _____

Step Ten: Facing the Bottom Line

You have now tested your business idea against the reality of securing work, meeting competition, handling clients, and making ends meet. You should know if you're likely to make a go of it or not. You should know if you can afford to go into full time freelance immediately or if you need to make a slow transition, keeping your salaried job while you develop a clientele. The figures are there to prove the worthiness of the endeavor.

    You've begun to get a feel for what it's like to go out and sell yourself to customers. Do you have what it takes to make the business flourish? And if you do, is it a truly viable idea, anyway?

If you can answer these questions with a confident (although suitably cautious) *Yes!* you are ready to make the break

One last exercise: Rewrite your business definition now. Using all the information you've gathered, make it as precise and clear as possible. See how much more substantial it is? How much more targeted? How much more easily you can sell yourself when you have a well-focused idea?

4 Making the Break:
Starting the Business

Sam opened the window and looked out across the tops of the tenements. He scratched at his stubbly chin. The world looked pretty bloodshot after he'd worked 18 hours straight, but he really was glad he'd opted for the thrill of victory instead of the security of defeat.

Every day he gave thanks that he'd walked out of that office. He could still see the looks on their faces when he'd begun packing up his stuff right in the middle of the biggest case of the year. His boss's shouts had been sweet music to his ears.

"Still," Sam said to himself ruefully, "I might not have had such a hard time getting my own agency started if the boss hadn't tried to blacklist me. Boy, that bridge went up in a blaze of momentary glory!"

Bridging the Gap

You are now ready to cross into the land of freelance. Your self-assessment and the preliminary business plan have given you the information you need to make the break with your past employment. It is worthwhile to try to make it as constructive a transition as possible. To many a freelance entrepreneur, the prime motive for being self-employed is to get free of the boss. As with Sam, the feeling is often so strong that when a

break finally comes, it's done without any consideration of its long-term effects.

To think it through logically, consider the first important question: Full-time or part-time freelance? Will
you keep your steady job (and paycheck) while you
cultivate your freelance work, or can you make the
change in one fell swoop? There are pluses and minuses
to either method. Let's look at them.

Breaking Away Slowly—The Part-Time Option

The Preliminary Business Plan has shown you if full-
time freelance is financially viable. But even if the
answer was "yes," you may want to make the move
more slowly. If the answer was "no," part-time freelance is your only option. It allows you to generate
clients and confidence. You can test the waters and
see how you react to the less-structured working situation of freelance employment.

There are basically three ways to begin freelancing
part time: (1) You retain your regular full-time job and
work after hours and on weekends to generate a freelance clientele; (2) You arrange for regular salaried
part-time employment and spend the rest of your time
on your freelance work; (3) If school, child care, or
other nonemployment obligations require your time,
part-time freelance as your only job can fill your schedule and pockets.

Part-time freelancing still demands that you deal with
the basic problems of launching a business. In order
to make part-time freelance successful, you must take
it very seriously. Unfortunately, if your bread and but-
ter does not depend on the success or failure of the
business, it is easy to get lazy and not put in the incredible effort it demands.

If you choose to keep your steady job, the money
you earn from freelance quickly becomes "a neces-

sity." Your life-style may expand to include that extra money; it happens to everyone. Then you find yourself in a bind. It gets less and less affordable to make the switch to full-time freelance and support yourself on that income only. The one solution is to bank all or most of the "extra" money so that you do not get used to an expanded income and so you can bankroll the transition to full-time freelance when that becomes appropriate.

Some people never do go entirely freelance; instead they shift to a part-time relationship with their current employer or find part-time salaried work in their field to provide a steady monthly base.

Dermott M. explains:

"I wouldn't give up my work with the publishing company for anything. When I told them I wanted to quit, they were sorry to have me leave. So they have been very generous and cooperative about letting me work for them part-time. I love publishing promotion. I'm good at it. I have several outside promotional clients too these days, but I'm not really interested in making any big machine out of it. I went to part-time freelance so that I could have the time to write fiction. It has worked out well. I can meet my monthly responsibilities and, with a tight schedule and discipline, do my writing as well."

Others see the choice of part-time freelance very pragmatically; for example, one editor (who asks not to be identified for obvious reasons) explains:

"My employer provides me with cost-free office space, a secretary, typewriter, phone, health insurance. As an editor, I am responsible for getting my work done. How and when is my decision; therefore, I do work on my freelance writing here, too, plus evenings and weekends. Someday I hope to be free of an office situation altogether, but until then, this is ideal. I wouldn't cut these ties until I was sure I could make enough to support me in the style to which I'm trying to become accustomed."

Crossing the Bridge

Once the decision has been made to change over to a full-time freelance life, there are many emotional issues that are as demanding of your attention as the financial ones are. You are moving into a whole new territory, with its own customs, styles, and rules. You must be as prepared to deal with the mood as with the money.

First of all, you are cutting yourself loose from the security and certainty of a regular job. Or, if you have not been working, you are putting yourself in a position that demands extra discipline and order where none existed. In either case, there is decompression time required. The initial euphoria that comes with starting a freelance project should not deceive you: You are not protected from the fear and the isolation that comes with the territory.

Your friends and family will have a hard time believing that you are "at work" if you are "just hanging out at home." They'll call to chat, ask you to run errands, expect you to be available to them in ways they would never dream of if you were at an office. Their lack of understanding of the seriousness of your work will undermine your feelings of positiveness and self-assuredness. So be prepared:

- Explain what your work is. Show that you take yourself seriously.
- Notify friends that if they call you at home while you are at work, you may well have to tell them you can't talk. Let them know ahead of time, so they are not hurt and so that you don't feel angry or guilty when you have to tell them.
- Explain to parents, children, and friends just how the business works and offer information about income and workload if it will help them understand and accept your new life-style. Don't get angry that you must justify yourself. Remember, what you are doing *is* out of the ordinary. Most people can't imagine how your new life operates.
- If you have children at home, you must establish

a routine that works for you and them. Some people thrive on the sound and energy of their kids around them. Others find it an unmanageable distraction. Recognize what works for you and then set up a structure that the kids can accept as routine.

Networking

Only a daredevil works without a net. When it comes to business, the smart person uses every possible resource. Networking is really a simple process of maintaining old contacts and associations, exploring old contacts that you've never used, and cultivating new ones. Networking is not manipulative, nor is it taking advantage of people. It is a way of establishing bonds that are as valid as friendships. You can think of them as *business-ships*.

A writer named Arthur gives the following example of how networking helped him:

"How did I get my first assignment in a national consumer magazine? Years ago, when I worked for a video company, I'd met the publisher of the magazine. Just last year, I was writing for trade magazines and needed to interview him for an article. 'Remember me? I'd like to interview you,' I told him when I called. Well, one thing led to another and he ended up asking me to write for his publication. I could have submitted proposals 'cold' and had no luck. But this old contact...it's what made the difference."

Arthur's example is apt, no matter what field you're in.

Building Your Bridges Behind You

It is of vital importance that you maintain your contacts from former jobs. If you are leaving full-time employment to go freelance, your boss can be of great help to you, if you handle the transition responsibly. Particularly if you are remaining in the same general field, you can benefit from his references, introductions, suggestions, and support. It is a measure of professionalism that such a transition is handled smoothly.

- Let your employer know of your reasons for leaving, well in advance.
- Explain to him (her) your reasons for wanting to go freelance.
- Ask for suggestions and advice.
- Don't hesitate to request help. Ask "Do you know anyone who might need my freelance services?"
- Don't overlook the possibility of continuing to work for your employer on a freelance basis.

Unless you are taking business away from your former boss, there is no reason why he should not be supportive and helpful to you.

Rekindle past contacts. You may have worked for someone several years ago who could use your services now. Call her up. Make an appointment. Explain what you are doing and see if she can provide you with information, references, or work itself.

Think back over people whom you have met socially, friends of friends or family, casual business acquaintances who may help with information or work. When possible, approach them by using the name of a third party (with that person's permission): "This is Joan Smith. I met you through James Steele. I am now running a catering service and wondered if I might come to see you at your restaurant. I am interested in asking you some questions about the food business and seeing if you might help me generate a list of potential clients."

Don't hesitate to make that phone call. It's not pushy, it's good business. People are usually delighted to help out. They are flattered. And as long as you don't come on as a needy, confused person, they will be glad to deal with you as one professional to another.

Developing Hidden Contacts

When you are starting to build your network, some of
your most valuable contacts will probably come through
people whom you seek out for information and support—not for work. You need to learn how to form
business relationships with people of whom you do not
directly ask anything. Sometimes it is appropriate to
directly request referrals or work. But often a business
lunch where you talk generally about your business
and open up a communication with another person in
your field is even more valuable. You want that person
to become aware of you and your work. Then in the
future that person might say to a third party, "Hey, I
know so-and-so, who is doing just what you need. Give
her a call." The results are not immediately measur-
able, but are valuable nonetheless.

Spreading Your Net

How can you meet people whom you have no way of
meeting socially or through business contacts? It's
tough to do this, but important to make the effort. If,
for example, you are considering becoming a shopping
advisor—a person who helps men and women plan and
purchase their wardrobes—you need to get to know
the store managers, designers, buyers, and sales reps
in your area. You need to know what lines will be
available for the coming seasons. You need a good
working relationship with the stores. (Remember, it is
to their financial advantage, too.) Therefore, you must
find out who these people are and make contact with
them. This is a two-part process.

First, do your research. Make a list of all the stores
in your area. Call manufacturers and get their reps'
names. Track down local designers and tailors. Break
your lists down by price and quality. You should have
a firm idea of the market you are going after. Some

stores will be of no interest to you, because they are outside that market. Go to the stores and see what lines they carry. Call the stores' personnel departments and ask for the names of the buyers for the various departments.

Second, make contact. Write a business letter introducing yourself and explaining your business concept. State clearly that in one week you will follow up the letter with a phone call, and that you hope to make an appointment to see them. Then call, and keep calling until you get through.

Remember, people don't mind if you call several times. It seems like much more of an intrusion to you than it does to them.

Whatever business you are starting, use this two-part plan to generate new contacts.

Letting the World Know

The Name Game

Children, pets, bands, and businesses...Oh! The terrible trouble we have choosing names. Some sound too serious, some too vague, some are catchy but silly. Friends and relatives call up with endless suggestions. You hate them all. So you think, "I'll just use my own name."

Well, Jerry Green Portrait Photography might work well enough, but Sylvia Tompkins Designs just isn't specific enough. Jerry Green's business name states exactly what he does. But Sylvia Tompkins does not explain what she designs. There is no way of knowing if she does graphic design, interior design, or dress design. When it comes to choosing a name, there are no absolute dos or don'ts. One very successful franchising business in New York is called Alaska Mama! The Beatles did just fine, even though, as John Lennon said, they could just as well have been called "Shoe"! There are, however, some guidelines that might prove helpful:

- Choose a name that fits your business attitude. A serious, corporate-sounding name such as "Entertainment Planners Service" may sound appealing to business clients who need to hire catering help. But for private parties, it is not a name that conveys fun. "First Course Caterers" or "Parties Perfect" has a much lighter, more festive tone.
- Keep the name short; use a subtitle if needed. There are exceptions "Marx and Hegel Lox and Bagels Dialectical Delicatessen" and "A Clean Well-Lighted Place for Books" are two San Francisco firms that have effective long names. But generally speaking, less is more. "Private Shopper: A Personal Buying Service," or "Greenleaf: Office and Home Plant Care" are two good examples of effective short names with subtitles.
- When using initials or a logo as a name, print the complete name somewhere on all letterhead and promotional material. SMP, Inc. is the name of an editorial service. "Smith, Morris and Persky Editorial Services" appears under the logo to provide clear identification of the meaning of the initials and the scope of the business itself.

Spreading the Word

It is essential to get together an effective promotional package to launch your new venture. This can include brochures, posters, advertisements, mailings, samples of your work, and letters of recommendation.

In all promotional literature, remember: You are judged on the appearance and tone of your correspondence. It is of utmost importance that it be professional quality and that it set out your services clearly and effectively. It can be costly to have material typeset and printed, but a roughly mimeographed or Xeroxed letter is not a cost-saving device; you spend less but get less in return. Mailings should contain:

- The name of the company
- The address
- The telephone number

- A brief paragraph explaining the spirit and scope of the business
- A list of services you provide
- Some indication of price, although listing specific costs is not advisable. Consider targeting audiences by using phrases like "cost savings," "highest quality for the economically minded," or "for those who demand the very best" and "an exclusive service for a special market," depending on which you plan to serve.

Perfecting Your Pitch

Once you have decided it's time to create your own promotional package, you want to target your mailings to potential clients and find ways of making your general services appeal to the specific needs of future customers.

If, for example, you are trying to get a small music publishing firm as a client for your public relations service, you need to know *whom* that company has in its catalogue, *how* they pitch their songs, *what* their image is in the business, *why* they could use a new approach (yours), and *where* you would try and generate publicity.

These specific questions can only be answered if you have a ready knowledge of the music business. If you don't, then pitch your public relations services elsewhere! To run a P.R. company, you must know more than how to write a press release and use contacts in the press and media.

Perfecting your pitch is in fact a fine-tuning process that calls for basic knowledge, some research, and creative thinking that demonstrates to your potential clients that you will service them. It doesn't matter if you want to tend someone's garden, decorate his apartment, or write his press release. You have to be able to anticipate and fill his needs.

Follow-through and contact are the next important steps. Once you have sent an informational package pitching your services, you must follow up and make an appointment to get together. This is fast-thinking time! You have managed to get in the door. Now you want to stay in!

You must be flexible. You must know your bottom line.

You want work—almost any work, as long as you don't lose money doing it; therefore, you must be prepared to adjust your proposed program to suit the client's needs and financial wherewithal without selling yourself short.

Remember, there are worse things than not getting a job—really. If you make a good presentation and have good rapport with the client, he or she may use you some other time. But if you land a job that will inevitably make you angry because it pays too little or demands too much, you'll end up alienated and probably won't ever work for that client again. So keep the long view. (For detailed information on negotiations and contracts, see Chapter 8.)

You are now officially the proprietor of your own business. It's time to set up your office.

5 Setting Up an Office

*The elevator ran, occasionally, and the electricity
and phone were finally turned on. Sam had an office. Well, he called it an office, but there was nothing in the two small rooms that could prove it to
anyone else.*

*"Gotta get some order in here," he said to him-
self. "Wish I could hire someone else to do it. Some
short-skirted, willing kid who'd think I was doing
her a favor by paying her too little and working her
too hard. But that comes later. For now it's just
me and the file drawers." Carefully, he put the pint
bottle under B for Bourbon, smiled, and felt that
he'd made a big step toward getting organized.*

Every freelancer needs an office. No matter if you sit
at a desk all day writing stories, run a day care program, do landscaping, or have a magic act, you have
to have some set place to work from: a place that lets
you plan and supervise your business. Where you work
has an impact on how you work. This is particularly
true for a freelancer, since an efficient office setup
establishes both the psychological structure and the
physical order that encourage good management.

You probably won't need (or want!) an office like
Sam's. But even if you do, it may be difficult to afford
an out-of-the-house office at first. Some businesses
demand it—but for the most part, you are better off
not assuming the additional overhead of paying rent

55

on a separate office at first. Later, when you've got money to burn, it's another story.

Establishing a Businesslike Spirit

When you go freelance, you are unmoored from the external support of "going to work." You are lucky if you commute from one room to the next. Many freelancers do not even have a separate room in their house to call an office. Because of this, it is often difficult to establish a sense of urgency about getting to the office on time. There is no clear line between just hanging out and working.

Millions of potential freelancers have gotten the germ of a business idea and then rushed out to get expensive stationery, rubber stamps, and file cabinets, in the attempt to establish a businesslike spirit with expensive props. Beware! This often indicates a kind of panic and lack of inner confidence that can doom even the best business idea. Far cheaper and more effective are the three simple steps below.

Designate a Permanent Work Area

Establish an office apart from the rest of the household. Don't use an area that doubles as the dining table. You need some permanent place to work, no matter how small and tucked-away.

Establish Minimum Office Hours

You can usually do your work, in part at least, at any time. But you should be available to make and receive business calls and set up appointments during regular working hours. Although you might want or need to get to work earlier, make it a point never to start work later than 10 a.m. Take a lunch break of one to two hours. This gives you time to have lunch appointments, run errands, and unwind. Get back to work in the afternoon for at least four hours. Set minimum standards and stick to them. If your business takes you out of the house, make sure that you have an answering machine or answering service to take calls. Don't let friends, children, or spouse answer your business phone.

Get Yourself Ready to Work

Initially, at least, make the effort to get dressed and pulled together in the morning. You may not have to take the care or time that you needed when you went out to an office, but you need to feel ready to face the day's work. Getting dressed and well groomed is a good psychological booster. (Admittedly, one of the pleasures of a freelance life is being able to sit in your robe with a cup of coffee while you make your morning calls or get a project started, but this can make it hard for you to really feel you are "at work" until you have firmly established your business regime.)

These may seem to be simple pointers to follow. But be warned: they are not. The temptation to say, "I can do that later" or to enjoy the freedom of having no boss but yourself, makes procrastination the first deadly sin of freelance.

General Office Setup

Every freelancer needs an office of some kind; however, different types of enterprises require different setups. Let's look at two.

The Out-of-the-House Business

If you actually perform your job only when you're "on location" out in the world, then your office serves as a launching pad. It is a place you stop in at the beginning and end of every day to make future plans, review current work, and record financial information. You need a desk, files, accounting systems, and planning systems just as any "office" freelancer, but you don't need an environment that is pleasant enough for spending 8 to 10 hours a day in.

What do you need? More than anything, you need

a system for receiving calls and keeping client contact current while you are out of the office.

Your answering service or machine is your lifeline. You must be able to call in throughout the day to see if there is any business you need to attend to. Don't let children, spouse, or friends answer your phone while you're absent, unless they can do it in a totally professional manner.

More than any other type of freelance business does, you may find yours needs part-time office help, an actual warm body to take calls, track you down, transmit information, and keep the business running while you're working. Don't take on an extra person before you can actually afford it—the cost of paying someone else must be met by the increased work he or she can generate for you, otherwise you're losing money. However, you may find that missed jobs and chances happen too often when you're away from the phone.

If you are going to hire someone, I suggest that you look for a college student who will work for a reasonable hourly wage on a part-time basis.

Office Freelancing

If you are a freelancer who runs an "office" business—for example, a writer, photographer in a studio, designer, or editorial or typing-service person—you may find that you spend 8 to 12 hours a day in your office.

Your actual physical setup becomes vitally important. Not only must you have a desk, files and an accounting system that works, you must also find it comfortable and aesthetically pleasing to remain in one spot for that length of time. You need to provide the following for yourself:

- A desk. This can be any surface that is large enough to accommodate papers, typewriter, desk-top files, and general office supplies. You can use a hollow-core door on top of filing cabinets, or an "official" desk; it matters not.

- A desk chair. Make this a top priority. If you sit for hours, you must have a comfortable chair. A straight-backed dining room chair will make it hard to sit at your desk. Particularly important is that the chair have an upholstered seat, so that the edge of it does not cut into your legs.
- Good lighting. Eliminate any external causes of fatigue or strain. Good lighting is vital.
- An adjacent reading chair. If you have a second, comfy chair available in your work area, you can give yourself a change of scene (it really helps!) without leaving the office. So often freelancers will get up from their desk for a break and end up washing the dishes. It is too easy to get sidetracked, so keep yourself in your work area as much as possible.
- A telephone on your desk. Don't have your phone across the room. If necessary, have the phone company change the location of one of your house phones. Again, you don't want to have to leave your office area to make or receive calls. It's inconvenient *and* the temptation to stay out of the office can be very strong.
- Special additional touches. Your work area should be pleasing to the eye as well as practical. Added plants, flowers, pictures on the wall, special objects all make it seem more comfortable. Take the time to make it a place you want to spend your time in—not just somewhere you have to be.

General Office Systems

Both in-office and on-location freelancers must have effective management systems for running their businesses. It doesn't matter what sort of enterprise you run, you must plan your work schedule, make goals, and set priorities. Written out, as follows, these procedures seem a little compulsive, but once you integrate them into your daily routine, they do not take any extra time or thought—in fact, they save both.

Basic Management Systems

Generate to-do lists in order to guide your work flow.

Daily: On 5 × 8 file cards, keep a running list of calls, errands, and projects to be done each day. By the end of each working day, your next day's list should be complete. Make it the first thing you look at each morning. Date the cards. Check off to-dos as they are completed. Transfer undone work to the next day's card.

Weekly: Each Friday sit down and map out the general work for the next week. Estimate the number of days each project will take. Use a regular wall calendar to record the information. This will help you to get a sense of what days are crowded with work commitments and what days can be used to make new contacts and secure new work.

Monthly: Set goals for each month. Write these into your daily appointment book. For example, "Make contact with eight clubs or organizations to discuss catering their dinners. Goal: Secure two definite contracts." List names and phone numbers of each.

Filing Systems

A well-organized filing system can make the difference between efficiency and chaos in any business. It is the easiest and fastest way to keep on top of your work. Basically, it should contain three sections: reference, ongoing work, and future prospects.

Reference File: This section of your filing system contains tear sheets, potential sources for ideas, clippings, pictures, business advice articles.

Set up a file for each reference category. If you are developing a reference file, break it down into specific areas. I knew a graphic designer who had a picture and type reference file that filled three filing cabinets and contained folders on everything from African animals to xylophones.

Ongoing Work File: Each client should have his or her own file. (You may want to break it down into two—one for the project, the other for correspondence, bills, and phone log.)

On the top of each file, list the name of client, all people you deal with, and their phone numbers. On the inside of the file itself, make a phone log. Each time you call the client, pull the file and make a note of the date and what was discussed. Each time he or she calls you, do the same. That way you have an infallible record of your ongoing communications. In the file, keep copies of all correspondence sent or received. Contracts, invoices, and records of payments should also be included.

The project folder should contain all your work—lists of what you did, samples of proposals, ideas you've jotted down and, when applicable, the final product.

Future Work File: These files contain names of prospective clients, contacts, and projects. Leads that you come across, ideas for expanding the business, and new areas of work—each requires its own folder. One of the problems faced by freelancers is continuity of work. When you are absorbed in an ongoing project, you don't have much time to cultivate your next job. By keeping a careful filing system at your fingertips, you can make the time to call prospective clients and develop new projects as efficiently as possible.

Telephone Book

A freelancer's telephone is the lifeline to the outside world. In addition to keeping a running phone log in each client folder, you must have a good business phone book or Rolodex in which you enter the numbers of every contact you make or hear about, references, and local stores and businesses you deal with. Note: When making business calls, find out all secretaries' and receptionists' names. They really do control access and you should be careful to cultivate a good telephone relationship with them.

Organizing the Desk Top

Once you've got all your files in order, there is still the problem of managing the piles of paper that accumulate every day on the top of your desk. Many of these papers are needed day after day during the course of a project and you don't want to file them away—not yet, anyway. If you have more than one project going at a time, the potential for chaos increases geometrically; therefore, you need to have a desk-top system.

Open-top vertical files work better than wire baskets, because you can actually see what's piling up; but it is really a matter of personal preference. I suggest that you have a separate file or basket for each job. Keep finished work separate from work in progress. And make it a point to clear papers off your working surface and place them in your desk-top files whenever you are done working.

As for pens, pencils, carbon paper, paper clips, and other office miscellany, you can pick up an inexpensive desk organizer at any stationery store. It is the little clutter that makes a desk a battle zone if not properly handled.

Gizmos—Necessary Glitz

The barrage of technological gizmology that comes at us from all sides is overwhelming. But it is not all hype. Some of it is really essential for efficient business management.

The basics are: a good typewriter, one that will take a film ribbon; an answering machine or service; and a calculator.

The typewriter is obviously essential. If you don't have one, it is possible to get a fine electric typewriter on a rental/purchase plan, so you don't have to spend too much cash up front. Shop around. Good deals on used machines are also available.

An answering machine or service is another essential. When you are out of the office on appointments or errands, your business must still be "open." If you have only one phone line for business and social calls, an answering machine or service is particularly vital. Make it a point to return all business calls promptly. If possible, get a machine that you can call into to get your messages while you're out of the house. Another phone plus is "call waiting." It lets you know when someone is calling you when you are talking on the line. This is an economical way to have two phone lines. It is available in almost all areas and helps keep your line from being "busy" when you are talking on it.

A calculator is indispensable. If possible, get one with a tape printer attached. When doing your books and keeping running totals, it saves time and helps insure accuracy. If you are discussing prices on the phone, it lets you come up with quick, accurate estimates.

Office Stationery

As for the signs and symbols of a proper office, there are two equally valid schools of thought. Stationery, invoices, cards, rubber stamps, etc. are all wonderful to have. With your business name printed boldly across the top, they convey a sense of "officialness" to your written communications. They are, however, expensive and not altogether necessary. A finely typed invoice on standard bond will not lose you a client. Just make sure all your correspondence is professional quality: neat, legible, well organized.

On the other hand, in a world that trades on image as much as ours does, there are those who feel business stationery and invoices present a serious first impression, which works to your advantage when you are starting out.

I feel that if you can afford it, by all means get a full complement of printed business supplies. Remember to keep it simple. Rose-colored paper may seem attractive, but you are generally better off with white, beige, or subtle grayed stock. If you want color on your letterhead, use a Pantone ink in printing it.

Using Outside Help

All this talk about being resourceful, taking charge, and accepting responsibility should not make you think you can do everything yourself. Jerry S., accountant and business manager par excellence, has seen it all, from anxiety to audit. He sums up his advice on managing a business: "Do what you can to organize your business and then turn it over to someone who's a pro to handle the details. Don't go it alone!"

If, in addition to your own trade, you're your own accountant, lawyer, or assistant, you are asking too much of yourself—and asking for trouble! You are not required to be the master of all trades, just your own. So don't postpone finding reliable experts to help you set up and run your business.

Choosing an Accountant

As soon as your business is off the ground and there is some amount of money to account for (even if it's negative accounting), find an accountant and/or tax advisor. Ask others who work in your field about their accountants. Interview several to make sure they really know the particular ins and outs (otherwise known as "legal loopholes") of your business. Shop around!

Don't begrudge your accountant his or her fee! The accountant should charge you competitively with other accountants, but don't choose one simply because he or she is the cheapest. Once you have chosen someone, have him or her help you set up your books.

The accountant will tell you the specific categories of expenses that are deductible in your business, and how to record those expenses so that they are easy to evaluate and add up at tax time. Your accountant can even give you investment and tax-shelter advice, if you have enough money to require that.

Choosing a Lawyer

Good legal advice is invaluable. Unfortunately, good or bad, it can be very expensive, so you need to find the best you can afford and then use the advice wisely. If you are in a business that negotiates contracts for large fees on a regular basis, a lawyer is indispensable. Take it from me. For years I did my own negotiating. We are all civilized and fair human beings, after all. Why did I need to pay someone to handle a conversation with an editor that I could have handled just as easily? Why indeed?

The main reason: To keep the business relationship with clients from being tainted by disagreements about money.

Let your lawyer argue, be difficult. You can remain calm and friendly. And when you know your lawyer (agent) is good, you can be sure he or she will get you the best deal possible, something one is never quite sure of one's self.

As you see, the way you set up your office *and* the way you keep it running are a very accurate measure of your degree of professionalism. All freelancers flounder, experiment, and mess up in the beginning. But you can take it from those who've gone before you: the sooner you get your office and business in shape, the sooner you'll start enjoying your work.

"The only way to tame the beast—and business can be a beast—is to get organized." Tyler W., a freelance audiovisual writer, can laugh now, looking back. But he admits: "I learned the hard way. Now I keep my files in order and always have a lawyer look over my contracts. Early on I was stiffed on a really big writing project. I didn't have anything on paper—no correspondence, no contract. I couldn't get a dime I was due."

You don't need to have that happen more than once to learn, but try to avoid even once. It's not easy, but it's worth it. When it's well run, a freelance business and life is a great pleasure. You are free, self-sufficient, adventuresome. There is no one to blame for your failures but yourself. But, conversely, your successes are all your own, too.

6 The First Stage:
Managing the Business

The ashtray was filled to overflowing; crumpled papers clustered around the legs of the wooden deskchair; the dawn's gray haze barely permeated the smoke-filled office. It had been a long, hard night. It would be an even harder day if something didn't bring money in the door. Everything would be allright if someone would call with a job, if the phone company would grant an extension on the bill, if the secretary wouldn't quit just because her paycheck bounced. If, if, if.

He'd counted on better luck, believed in quicker results. He looked up at the words stenciled on the glass door to the hallway. There was little joy in them now.

SAM SPARK FREELANCER

Sam lit another cigarette. It tasted like dust.

If is the most dangerous word in a freelancer's vocabulary. It is also the most common. For it's an iffy business, this self-employed life, and so much seems to hinge on the unknowable future.

There are some steps you can take to manage the ifs, to fence them in, tamp them down, round them up, and, with any luck, throw them away. There is the short form: you can memorize the following five commandments and four deadly sins. There is the long form: you can set up a management system that helps you control the vagaries of your business. The first is more fun; the second more effective. Let's look at them both.

The Five Commandments

1. Get it in writing.
2. Balance thy budget.
3. Keep regular office hours
4. Don't get too grand.
5. Don't expect a vacation.

The Four Deadly Sins

1. Having a four-hour breakfast (much like the three-martini lunch).
2. Spending now, earning later (as in, "I'll buy that new typewriter now, on credit, and pay for it next month").
3. Believing in promises (such as "the check is in the mail," or, "I'll have a big job for you soon").
4. Avoiding unpleasant jobs (as in returning phone calls or figuring out exactly how you stand financially).

Developing a Management System

The key to running a well-managed business is the establishment of a system that provides an ongoing structure for processing all your financial and job-related tasks. For virtually all freelancers, this system is what is called a *sole proprietorship*.

A sole proprietorship is a business run by one person. Basically this means that you and your business are one and the same entity. Heavens knows, you may feel that way. But this is not simply a description of the psychological nature of your work! It is also a legal description of the financial and tax liabilities of the business.

In a sole proprietorship, all income earned is recorded as personal income. You deduct business-related expenses from your personal income to figure out your taxable income.

This is distinct from the tax situation in other forms of business management systems. The other systems—partnerships, corporations, subchapter S corporations, and professional service corporations—all have their own variations on this scheme.

Some of you may need or want to deal with these other forms of business. But for most of you, the sole proprietorship provides the easiest, most financially advantageous form. Let's explore it in detail. The other forms are reviewed briefly at the end of the chapter.

Are You a Candidate for a Sole Proprietorship?

- Are you self-employed? Yes! Otherwise you wouldn't be reading this!
- Do you earn less than $80,000 a year? Alas, most of you will also answer "yes."
- Do you run another business of any kind that is making a profit? I wish you were. But again, you probably are not. (If you are, see information about Subchapter S corporations.)
- Are you in this alone? Yes? No partners, silent or otherwise? Then you're sole-proprietorship material.
- Are you running a professional freelance business as an architect, doctor, or lawyer? Probably not—since those are not, strictly speaking, freelance businesses. If you are, however, see the section on page 90 about professional service corporations, for information that could save you a bundle.

So you run a business alone, make less than $80,000 a year, are not in a licensed profession, and do not run any other profitable businesses. Welcome to the world of sole proprietorship!

Even if you are a full-time employee of another business, you are self-employed in your freelance work. For tax purposes you run a sole proprietorship, since your income and expenses are earned and deducted within that enterprise. See page 72 for further explanation of allowable deductions.

Advantages of a Sole Proprietorship

A sole proprietorship provides you with:

- Sound accounting procedures. (All you have to do is follow them!)
- Maximum tax deductions.
- Minimum legal and accounting expenses.
- Easy-to-understand profit-and-loss and cash-flow projections.

Before you wade into the details of managing your new business, you have one easy decision to make: Are you going to run the business under an assumed name or not?

An assumed name may be anything from the simple to the ridiculous. For example, I would be running a business under an assumed name if I chose to call myself *Kalia Lulow Productions*, instead of simply *Kalia Lulow*. Adding the word "Productions" to my name, and receiving payment from clients made out to Kalia Lulow Productions, means that I must set up a separate checking account, which I am authorized to use to receive and issue checks made out to that name. To do this I must:

- Obtain Legal Form #201: "Certificate of Conducting Business Under an Assumed Name for Individual." It is available through your county clerk, at large stationery stores, and at some banks.
- Set up a checking account under that name at your bank. Give the bank a copy of your certificate. The bank will provide you with authorization to sign company checks.

Once you have set up a sole proprietorship under
an assumed name, you need to obtain a Federal Identification Number (FIN). This number is used for filing
taxes. (Those of you who run a sole proprietorship
under your own name continue using your social security number as identification.) To get a FIN:

- Contact your local IRS office and ask for the form.
- The form will ask for:
  - The name of your business.
  - Mailing address.
  - The month in which your fiscal year ends. (Make
    it December, since as a sole proprietor you and
    your business file the same tax return.)

Now that you have decided on a name, you are
ready to get the business rolling.

Running a Sole Proprietorship

The single most important business system you have
to set up is your accounting procedures. Not only are
you responsible for keeping track of income and expenses for your tax records, but you have a chance to
control the cash flow and make budgets if you keep
your books up to date and accurate.

There is so much to deal with: getting work; perfecting your trade, art, or craft; dealing with clients;
doing promotion. You may be inclined to let your
bookkeeping slide. Don't. I can't urge you strongly
enough. If you do, you'll just make life harder on yourself in the long run. On this one—believe me. And if
you don't want to believe me, believe the IRS. You
have to have good records to get all the business deductions you deserve. They'll nail you if you can't
substantiate your claims. And you have so many possible legitimate deductions—so many ways to get a tax
break—that you'd be a fool not to keep good records.
Enough said. You get the point, right?

Let's look at the monthly record-keeping systems
that any sole proprietorship should establish.

The Basic Ledgers—Monthly Record-Keeping Systems

Every month you are going to fill in two basic ledgers, recording cash, checking, and credit card business expenses. Then you're going to tally your income ledger in preparation for writing out your profit-and-loss statement, your cash-flow projections, and establishing your monthly budget.

Your basic ledgers will be your (1) Cash ledger and (2) your checking and charge card ledger.

You set up your ledger for two reasons: to keep track of how and why you spend your money and to document expenses that are valid business deductions when you file your income tax return. To do this, you need a record of both your cash-paid expenses and check-paid or credit-card-paid expenses.

Both ledgers will record your expenses for the month. When keeping your records, don't be conservative. If you're uncertain about an item, include it anyway. Let your accountant tell you if something can be deducted or not. Don't censor yourself.

List of Deductible Business Expenses

According to the IRS, the following items are fully deductible as business expenses:

1. Office furniture, or equipment.
2. Business taxes (other than federal income tax).
3. Business rent and mortgage, and property taxes.
4. Business repairs to office.
5. Salaries and wages—to any temporary freelance assistants you might hire.
6. Business insurance, such as theft insurance, liability insurance, fire insurance.
7. Business-related legal and professional fees.
8. Commissions and referral fees.
9. Interest on business loans.
10. Auto expense, mileage, travel, taxi, and public transportation costs.

11. Promotion and advertising costs.
12. Dues to professional organizations, clubs, or unions. (Initiation fees are not deductible.)
13. Entertainment—the cost of business dinners, theater tickets, dinners at home, etc., during which business is conducted.
14. Professional books, magazines, etc.
15. Special clothing and uniforms (only if worn exclusively for work).
16. Education expenses, including seminars, that further your job-related skills for your present business, trade, or profession, and travel to classes, books for classes, fees, etc.
17. Freight and postage for any business mailings.
18. Business telephone—either a separate line or a percentage of your home phone bill; answering service charges.
19. Office and shop supplies.
20. Bank charges.
21. Cost of goods sold—if you sell a product, the cost of all materials and production are valid business expenses. (You pay tax on *profit per item*, not price received.)

Special business expenses deductions:

1. Golf, Tennis, and Club dues—in part.
2. Cost of participation in civic affairs as advertising. For example, sponsorship of a community activity, event or organization can be deducted as a public relations/advertising expense.

The following items are not deductible as business expenses:

1. Personal expenses.
2. Medical insurance; life insurance premiums.
3. Personal legal expenses or doctors' bills.

As you can see, the range of possible deductible expenses is vast. But remember that you are not interested in deductible costs alone. You want to know how much you spend every month to keep the business going, no matter how the IRS views those costs. Therefore you want your ledgers to be very detailed, covering all your business expenditures.

The Cash Ledger

The cash ledger is particularly important since you spend, in the course of a year, an enormous amount of money on little items for which you get no receipts and have no record other than your daily notation in your appointment book and your monthly tally in the ledger. A cash ledger will probably contain entries for the items listed below:

- General office supplies: paper, pens, typewriter ribbons, glue, invoices, Xeroxing, and whatever else you need to run the office. Remember, a light bulb that goes into your desk lamp is a business expense. Even flowers and plants used to decorate an office area qualify. Don't be reluctant here— let your accountant tell you if something is out of line.
- Specialized supplies: If you knit and sell homemade sweaters, then yarn is an expense. If you are a writer, yarn is a personal indulgence. So there are no rules here, just a rule of thumb: if you use it in business, deduct it.
- Reading material: Any journal or book that pertains to your profession is deductible. If you're a general writer, then anything goes. If you are a carpenter, you are limited to furniture design publications and craft papers.
- Postage: Anything you do to send your clients information or products is an operating cost.
- Transportation: The cost of using taxis and public transportation to and from appointments where you are trying to obtain or retain work is deductible. There is also an allowance for car travel. Keep records of miles driven and gasoline purchases. Your accountant will determine the amount of deduction available. Additionally, tips paid while traveling are business expenses.

- Entertainment: When you eat out with a client or potential client, your meal (and the clients meal too, if you pay for it) is a legitimate expense. Any cash outlay for theater or concerts should also be recorded.
- Cleaning services: If you must pay in cash to those who perform janitorial services for your business—window-washing, floor-waxing—try to get them to provide a receipt. If they won't, break down the expenses into $25 chunks and enter in your day book. (You aren't required to have receipts for cash expenses under $25.)
- Suggested additions: To take full benefit of good record-keeping, you may want to enter your personal nondeductible expenses as well. That way, you'll always know where the money has gone. So have a section for groceries, laundry, cosmetics, and the like. It's good to see how you allocate your funds so you can make choices about what to reduce if money is tight.

Sample Pages from a Cash Ledger

Office Supplies & Maintenance		Business Equipment	Reading Material
Date	Cost	Date Cost	Date Cost

Transportation	Travel	Entertainment	Postage
Date Cost	Date Cost	Date Cost	Date Cost

The Check and Charge Card

Each month when you get your bank statement, sit down with the cancelled checks or statement and your checkbook and log in those checks that pertain to business. The categories and set up are shown in text.

Sample Page from a Check and Charge Card Ledger

Item	Check Number and Date Written	Amount	To	For
Rent				
Phone				
Gas & Electric				
Professional or union dues				
Subscriptions to professional magazines				
Office equipment (from a $15 calculator to a $5,000 word processor)				
Office help & workers (including typing services, janitorial, messengers, any assistant)				
Gifts				
Advertising & promotion expenses				
Entertainment				
Miscellaneous				
CHARGE CARD EXPENSES: Travel				
Entertainment				
Supplies				

The Income Ledger

Once you've set up your basic monthly records, you will need a third, and—I hope—active ledger—your income record. This is where you enter all your earned income. Specify date received, from whom, amount, and work being paid for. Attach your deposit slips from the bank to the entry page.

Remember, you can go to jail for failing to report taxable income. If you claim excess expenses as deductions, you are simply assessed more money. There are enough tax advantages for the self-employed; there is no reason to lie about income.

A Taxing Situation

Now that you've got all three of these important record-keeping systems set up, let's look at how you will use them to calculate your taxes. As a sole proprietor, you have many tax breaks—possible deductions. Of course, nothing is easy when it comes to the IRS, so the trick here is figuring how much you can deduct legally, and without triggering an audit.

Jerry S. has watched many of his clients go from struggling careers in music and other arts to being successful heads of their own freelance companies. It is his advice and savvy that helps them hold on to the money they make and plan for the future. He comments:

"Your job is to practice your talent. Mine is to help you continue. Any good accountant should feel the same. You can't possibly know everything you should about taxes, investment, budgeting, etc. You have to know enough to choose an accountant wisely and supervise what he does. You must be able to present your financial records in an accurate fashion. But unless you are really a trained business person, you have to hire helpers."

Most of you will be conducting your business out

of your home. Some, like Sam, may be able to afford
the luxury of an official office, but that is rare. If you
do have an official business address, complete with
phone, electricity, and rent, you can deduct all those
costs in their entirety from your gross income. They
are pure business expenses.

However, if you run a business out of the house,
you cannot deduct *all* your rent, utilities, maintenance,
and telephone bills as business expenses. You *live* there
too! And your business does not take up the entire
house or every moment of the day. So *how* do you
figure the cost of running a business out of your house?
And *why* do you want to figure it anyway?

The first question? We'll get to it in a minute. (I told
you it wasn't easy.) The answer to the second question—Why figure the costs?—is to find out what your
overhead is, that is, the cost of keeping the business
alive. In that way you can accurately determine your
monthly budget and evaluate how much income the
business has to make before it turns a profit. Another
reason for calculating the cost of running a business is
to allow you to take the deductions you are entitled to
when you file your income tax returns.

Now, back to how to calculate the cost of running
a business out of your house.

Using Schedule C of the 1040 form, you enter your
business income and expenses as described below.

Fixed Expenses and Deductions

Rent or Mortgage Payments. If you conduct your business at home, you may deduct the expenses of renting
that area allocated to business. Your right to such a
deduction is unquestionable, but the *amount* is open
to interpretation. In the strictest interpretations, the
room—or area—designated must be used solely for
business. If you claim one room of a three-room apartment as an office, but your bed is there, then technically you can't deduct the whole room. Just make sure
that your room could withstand an audit. If so, then

you have a 33% deduction. Work with your accountant to determine a reasonable allocation.

The IRS's standards are:

1. The home office must be the taxpayer's principal place of conducting THAT particular business. In a recent appeals case in tax court (see E. Curphey 73TC/No. 61 CCH/Dec36,753), CPA Jerry S. won a decision for a college professor who had a salaried teaching job and also conducted a sole proprietorship from his home. The court allowed the deduction of a percentage of his rent because the home-based office was *the primary location of that business*. Therefore, those conducting a business while maintaining *another* job may take the deduction too. (To deduct a home-based office which is used to transact the same business that you do at another office is usually not permitted, however. Consult with your accountant about such deductions and the latest IRS rulings.)

2. The home office must be used frequently and exclusively as a place where work is done and where clients come. *Exclusive use* means that that room or area of a room must be used only for business. In a recent ruling, the tax court found that a partition between an office area and the rest of a room is not necessary for that section of the room to meet the exclusivity test. However, only that portion of the room is deductible—not the whole room.

Let's look at an example: Susan uses 20% of her home for business. She grossed $20,000 through that business. She pays $6,000 a year in rent. She can deduct for business rent $1,200 ($6,000 × 20%) from her income of $20,000. This brings her taxable income to $18,800. As she subtracts other deductible expenses, her taxable income will get lower and lower.

Direct Expenses for Maintenance of a Home Business. Any expense incurred to repair, paint, maintain, or improve the office is completely deductible.

Indirect Expenses for Maintenance of a Home Business. When making general improvements to the whole house, such as painting the exterior, fixing the furnace, or the like, the amount that can be allocated to the business is the same as the percentage of the whole house that is defined as the office (in Susan's case, 20%). Therefore, if it cost $500 to fix Susan's furnace, $100 is deductible as a business expense.

Allocation of Utility Costs. You can write off the cost of electricity, water, or gas that is used by your business. For example: if your yearly electric bill is $500 and you claim you use 20% of your home for business, then $100 of your yearly electric bill is a business deduction.

Allocation of Telephone. All long distance business-related calls are deductible. In addition, the message unit charge for local business calls is deductible. The basic monthly phone charge can be deducted in part, but the basic charge that covers your personal phone use is not deductible. If you have a phone that is used only for business, then it is fully deductible. And remember, when you are out of the house, business calls from pay phones are legitimate deductions.

Capital Investments. The cost of big items—machinery, office equipment, office furnishings etc.—can be treated in two ways:

—Depreciated, where the cost of the item(s) are spread over more than one year, and part deducted each year until the initial cost is recovered, or

—Expensed, where the cost of the item(s) is deducted in the year in which it is placed in service, up to a maximum of $5,000 (1982 and 1983) or $7,500 (1984). For example, if an $8,000 word processor is purchased for business use, the first $5,000 may be expensed, and the remaining $3,000 depreciated over several years. The total amount you can write off in one year is $5,000, regardless of the number of items. An investment credit is also allowable in the first year for items which are depreciated. Check with your accountant about this and the new accelerated depreciation system.

Figuring Business Overhead

To accurately determine how much your business costs to run, you need to add up your allocated expenses. An allocated expense is that percentage of your rent, phone, electricity, automobile etc. that is deductible as a business expense. For example, Susan can deduct 20% of her home for business. That means that 20% of her monthly rent of $500 (or $100) is business overhead. Similarly, she spends $100 a month on gas and electricity. Her business cost for utilities therefore is $20. These figures, plus other allocated costs for phone maintenance and the like, give her the monthly overhead she must meet to pay for running the business.

Facing an Audit

So you go by the book—more or less—and your records are in reasonable shape and still you get audited. Don't panic; as long as you've reported all your income, nothing too bad can happen. Remember, the IRS has to prove you wrong. The burden is on them. And while you do *not* want an antagonistic environment with your auditor, there are some subtle tricks to use.

What Happens When You're Audited.

- If you are chosen for an audit, you will receive an audit letter. It states exactly what is being examined. THEY MAY NOT GO INTO OTHER AREAS AT THE TIME OF THE INITIAL AUDIT without prior notice, so, if the IRS questions your travel deductions, bring in receipts or journal entries.
  Upon receiving the audit letter, contact your accountant immediately. He or she can, if necessary,

reschedule the audit appointment, and together you can prepare and develop a strategy.

Generally it is not advisable to go to an audit alone, for it's easier for the IRS to take advantage of a nervous taxpayer. It's no time to act like a pioneer.

- Try to go to the audit in the afternoon if possible. The appearance of a Schedule C audit guarantees a long process and your examiner wants to get home on time!

- Present your receipts and records so that it takes some effort to wade through them. Staple cash receipts to the pages of your day book so that it is hard to sort them out. You can—although it's potentially unpleasant—dump all your receipts in a pile without any presorting. If it doesn't make the examiner mad, it will certainly discourage him. On this and other procedural techniques, follow your accountant's advice. This is a tip I got from several sources, but it is not universally advised.

- Don't capitulate when you think you're right. Tell the auditor you disagree and you're going to take it to appeal. It is your right and privilege.

Cautions. Experienced accountants agree that there are different grades of justice for different people and that three auditors would come up with three conclusions from the same material. Therefore, you must be prepared for the worst (which means you will file an appeal), but act like you expect the best, showing you are confident that you have not done anything wrong.

So, bearing all this in mind, collect those receipts and keep those records. You've got nothing to lose but the shirt off your back!

Other Taxes

When you worked for someone else, your federal income tax, state tax and social security tax, are usually deducted automatically by your employer from your paycheck. When you are self-employed, *you* are responsible for paying these taxes, plus a few others yourself.

Estimated Taxes

As the sole proprietor of your business, you will have to pay a quarterly federal and state tax based on the income that you expect to earn that year, since no employer is withholding a part of the monies you earn. If you do not pay your estimated tax on time, or underestimate your tax, you may be subject to a penalty charge. If you are unsure about your projected income, then one way to avoid the penalty is to cover the prior year's total tax. File quarterly, using the IRS Estimated Personal Tax Form, 1040ES. Ask your accountant for further details on how to estimate your income, or any other aspects of estimated tax that are confusing to you.

Social Security or Self Employment Tax

You are also responsible for self employment tax on Form 1040, Schedule SE, if your *net earnings* are over $400 on your Schedule C. As a sole proprietor, you must pay 9.35% on your net income over $400, and up to $35,700. In determining your total Federal Tax, income tax and social security tax are added together.

State Sales Tax

Everyone operating a sole proprietorship (with or without a company name) who sells a taxable product or goods to a client must collect sales tax and pay it to his/her state government. State to state the law differs, but if you sell anything that you would pay sales tax on at a store, you too must tax your customers. Graphic artists, photographers, craftspersons, even caterers—all are generally liable.

Four times a year, you will have to provide an accounting of your sales and the tax collected, and pass it along to the government. So in pricing and billing, make sure you include sales tax—otherwise it's going to come out of your pocket! For the proper forms, contact your State Department of Taxation.

State Tax Resale Number

You may also qualify for a state tax resale number, which exempts you from paying sales tax on items you purchase to produce your product. The end product itself will be taxed when you then sell it to a client. Your state Department of Taxation will provide information.

Unemployment Tax Numbers

Technically, all businesses, whether or not they expect to have employees, should contact their State Department of Labor to find out if they are officially exempt from the unemployment tax obligation. Ask your lawyer or accountant if he or she believes this to be necessary in your state and with your particular business.

Other Helpful Accounting Systems

Having set up your monthly ledgers, determined your fixed overhead costs, and dealt with your tax obligations, it's time to look at some accounting systems that are designed to help you keep control of your business.

The Monthly Profit-and-Loss Statement

Your monthly profit-and-loss statement (P&L) is for your benefit only. It tells you where you are. It helps you plan for the next month. Over time, these statements will reveal trends and business cycles. You'll be able to have a better understanding of cash flow.

Basically, the P&L looks like this:

Monthly Profit-and-Loss Statement

Fixed Expenses:	$ _____
(rent, phone, etc.)	
Cash Expenses:	$ _____
Credit Card Expenses:	$ _____
Check Expenses:	$ _____
(do not include those already listed under "Fixed Expenses")	
Total Expenses:	$ _____
Total Gross Monthly Income	$ _____
Difference Between Total Expenses and Total Monthly Income (+ or −)	$ _____

Well, there it is in gruesome black and white! Have you made it?

Month to month, you may have a profit and then a loss. Obviously, you use that profit to cover your losses. But on the P & L itself, you do not make this adjustment. To provide an overview, place an extra column on the P & L headed "Year to date."

It might look like this:

Year-to-Date Profit-and-Loss Statement

June totals were: Profit, $2,300.	
July totals were: Losses $1,400.	Year to date: Profit $ 900.00
Aug. totals were: Losses $ 200.	Year to date: Profit $ 700.00
Sept. totals were: Profit $ 635.	Year to date: Profit $1,335.00

The year-to-date profit-and-loss statement lets you know just how you're doing. If the profit accrues, come December you may want to make a tax-deductible expenditure in your business, or invest in a tax-deferred retirement plan, to lower the taxable income. Talk this over with your accountant.

Cash-Flow Projections

Budgeting your income—which invariably comes in large chunks or not at all—is the single hardest management task you'll face as a freelancer. First, you work so hard, and for so long, that when there is money you feel you deserve to indulge and reward yourself. Second, even without those little extravagances, planning cannot predict all future expenses and cash requirements, either personally or for your business. What to do? Plan and pray. It isn't an entirely satisfactory solution, but it's all you've got.

Tracking Cash Flow

From month #1 of your business, you should use your monthly profit-and-loss statements to help you project cash flow into the next one to three months. (Three is ideal, but there might not be enough cash to flow, so

---

Cash-Flow Chart

Cash available, from P&L Statement (+ or −):   _____

Accounts receivable (definite income
   this month):   _____

                    TOTAL CASH AVAILABLE (+ or −):   =======
Fixed expenses (overhead):   _____

Expenses anticipated for conducting
   business, serving accounts,
   filing work orders: _____

Personal Expenses: _____

                               TOTAL EXPENSES: =======
The difference between CASH AVAILABLE and
   CASH NEEDED (+ or −):   =======

go with the time interval that you can manage.) This is a way to predict shortfall and to plan for the amount of new work that you MUST generate to survive.

Monthly Budget

Based on your P & L statement and cash-flow projection for the coming month, you can set up your budget for each subsequent month, as is shown in the monthly projected budget below.

Monthly Projected Budget

A. *Expenses:*

Fixed Expenses (next month): _____

Personal Expenses (next month): _____

Billable Business Expenses (that is, money you must lay out to do a job but will be repaid when you bill your client for expenses.) _____

Non-billable Business Expenses (that is, expenses you must incur to conduct business and cannot pass directly on to any client. Such costs as paper, pens, typewriter ribbon, essential office supplies.) _____

TOTAL EXPENSES NEXT MONTH: ══════════

B. *Cash Available:*

Profit for Year to Date (see last month's P&L Statement): _____

Income due this month: _____

TOTAL CASH AVAILABLE: ══════════

SUBTRACT TOTAL A FROM TOTAL B (+ or −): ══════════

Limiting Personal Expenses

Your budget includes both business and living expenses. If you come up with a negative income, you will have to reallocate personal living expenses and get by on less. Your business budget is rather fixed.

1. Add up only all business expenses under "Expenses." In other words, omit Personal Expenses from the total.

2. Subtract #1 (all business expenses) from Cash Available total.

3. Divide money left over (I hope there is some) by four. That gives you your weekly personal allowance available.

4. Compare weekly money available (which you have just calculated in #3) with minimal personal requirements.

5. If there is a shortfall, examine personal expenses to see how they can be cut. Unfortunately, you must continually sacrifice yourself to your business. If you cut out movies, you may pay for a printing job. If you spend nothing on clothes, you may be able to take a client to lunch and secure more work.

6. When there is a surplus, do not absorb it, but put it into the next monthly cash-flow projection. Balance income and expenses there, and see what you have. Any left over? Go for the third month's projection. Spread out the "extra" over as long a period of time as possible.

A freelancer must keep tabs on cash flow at all times. Otherwise, the boom-and-bust cycle continues endlessly and there is never a feeling of balance or security.

You must know when, within the month, you can afford to spend money. Some bills may have to be delayed until week three, so that income will have arrived to cover expenses. Sometimes you can chart out a rough schedule, week by week. Although this is where you must rely on seat-of-the-pants financial juggling, it is good to think it through and try to devise a plan so you know when you are out on a limb.

Alternative Management Systems

Here is a brief look at the other options available to you when you choose a business structure. Each of these calls for the professional guidance and advice of a lawyer and accountant. Although there are kits available for do-it-yourself incorporation proceedings and partnership agreements, I advise you to get professional advice and assistance. If you can't afford it, you aren't ready anyway!

Partnership

A partnership can come about in two ways. One, you take a partner on as an investor who bankrolls you but does not participate in the actual work done. Or, two, you have a freelance partner who works with you as an equal in the production of your business. A partnership may exist in any *unincorporated* trade or business venture.

For your protection, an official and well-detailed partnership agreement *must be drawn up*. This is best done with the help of a lawyer. But you can do it yourself using the official legal Form #107, "Articles of Co-Partnership," available from Julius Blumberg, Inc., Law Blank Publishers, 80 Exchange Place, New York, N.Y. 10004. The points to be covered are:

1. Division of work responsibilities.
2. Division of financial obligations—money to be put into the business by each partner.
3. Division of profits and responsibility for losses and debts.
4. How a breakup of the partnership will be handled: buy-out plans, division of property, etc.
5. Title each partner holds.
6. Arbitration procedures.
7. How expansion will be handled.

When filing federal taxes, Form #1065, the Partnership form, must be filled out. It clearly sets out the distribution of profit and loss to each partner. Many partnerships are established for tax-shelter situations. That doesn't apply to you. However, your return does go into the same IRS "pot" as those more fancy-stepping financiers and 40% of all partnership returns are subjected to audit by the IRS!

Corporation

In a corporation, you do not personally accrue your profits and are not in most cases personally liable for suits against your company for negligence, default, or personal injury.

Some businesses in which the client traffic is heavy, such as a business with a store or office open to the public, need to protect themselves from suits. Insurance can cover this but does not, in and of itself, protect you from a personal suit. Incorporation does.

As for the tax advantages, unless you are generating a gross income of at least $80,000 per year, there are few pluses to incorporation. When you incorporate, you must pay not only an initial fee, but both corporate taxes, using IRS Form #503, and personal taxes (on the salary you pay yourself from the corporate account). You are liable for payment of the employer's share of Social Security and unemployment compensation, PLUS the FICA withholdings on your paycheck. The advantages to this become apparent only with a large income. The tax ceiling on corporate profits is 46%, while individuals can be taxed up to 90%.

The Professional Corporation or PC

A relatively new form of business organization, known as the PC, has been set up by the IRS to allow professionals to take advantage of tax breaks, retirement plans, and medical insurance plans that used to go only to regular corporations. Accountants, lawyers, and doctors are the most common professionals falling into this category. But architects, engineers, licensed masseuses, and the like also qualify. Check with your lawyer or accountant if you freelance in a "profession" to see if you should make this move.

Subchapter S Corporations

This is another friendly IRS creation designed to aid small business persons. A Subchapter S corporation can file with the IRS to obtain permission to be exempt from corporate income tax. All taxable income in a Subchapter S is accrued to the shareholders in the corporation (that's you), and you pay personal income tax on that money, much as a person in a partnership would do. The advantages are that you have the protection from personal liability that corporations provide. If you have an income from sources other than your Subchapter S business, the losses incurred in your "S" enterprise can be deducted as losses from your personal income from other sources. This is not true in a regular corporation. Therefore, if you are making a lot of money and set up a small business on the side, this form is probably good for you. If your Subchapter S business begins to make a profit, however, it may be to your advantage to dissolve it and form a regular corporation. This is a lot of high-level machination; if you are at this point, you definitely should have a lawyer and an accountant. They'll handle this!

7 Banking and Insurance:
Securing Your Business

The first big job—really big—had just walked in the door. Sam knew he should feel pretty good. The fee was enough to keep him going for six months— when the fee got paid, that is. But he knew that would take awhile.

"The check's in the mail"—he could already hear it.

The big question was, how was he going to survive between today and the time he finally got paid? His bank wasn't real fond of promises. He couldn't go to his new client and tell him he was starving and needed to get paid quickly. It just wouldn't sound professional.

This was the part of running his own business that Sam truly hated—the cash-flow crunch. Cash trickle, really, he thought, how can I get out of this one?

An entrepreneurial personality is not afraid of banks. They are a source of information and assistance, not an adversary! But few of us have a personal relationship with our banks these days. It is important that you take the time and effort to establish one. Get to know your bank manager, officers, and tellers. Present your business seriously. Set up structures for dealing with cash-flow problems and a line of credit *before you need it.*

Choosing A Bank

When it comes to choosing a bank for your personal and business affairs, the main consideration is the amount of attention you can get—as a customer and an individual. Savings and Loan Associations are one option: and with their new flexibility, they can provide you with checking, investment plans, loans, and a very full range of financial and personal services. Commercial banks no longer have an exclusive hold on such services.

For a small business, it does not make so much difference what type of bank you choose; it is the attitude that is of primary concern. Some commercial banks are getting very hostile to small depositors and do everything they can to discourage them from opening or maintaining accounts. This kind of abuse you don't need to pay for! And remember, *you* are paying for your banking services. You want a bank that takes the small business person seriously, as seriously as you take yourself. Therefore, if you are thinking of opening a new account, shop around. Talk to officers at various banks. Introduce yourself and your business. Explain what you are looking for from them and see how they respond.

The Business Statement

Your banker is your partner in securing credit and providing solutions to temporary financial crises in your business. To establish a business relationship, you must present yourself in a serious, businesslike way. The conventional way of introducing your business is to provide a business statement. This is a form that sets out your financial status, problems, future goals, and plans. In a sole proprietorship, this is less formal than it would be in a small business that sells and manufactures goods or retails products from a store. However, a two-page letter setting out your business will show that you are as serious about your endeavor as any more conventional entrepreneur. The business statement should answer these questions:

- What is your business definition?
- What is your profit?
- What costs (expenses) are a problem?
- What are your debts?
- What are your future assets (and future work)?
- What change (progress) has there been over time?

Below is an example of a business statement, one for John Doe Cleaners.

John Doe Cleaners—Business Statement

Income Last Year $18,500

Income This Year to Date 10,000

Projected Income, Rest of Year 15,000

Assets (Cash and Material) 6,500

Debts 2,200

Projected Business Expenses
(new equipment, etc.—whatever you foresee
as necessary to conduct your business) . . . . $4,100 (Total)

Business Definition: <u>John Doe Cleaners is a full service house-keeping business specializing in providing small businesses and private individuals with ongoing maintenance of their premises, including upkeep of wood floors, and heavy-duty cleaning.</u>

BUSINESS GOALS: <u>I want to expand my services by purchasing a carpet-cleaning unit, professional quality window-cleaning equipment, and an electric floor-waxer.</u> This will allow me to contract for additional jobs and expand my staff to include one additional full-time hourly employee.

You should have a rough idea of what you are asking for. Although you will be working *with* your banker to discover the right solutions for you, you must be well-informed.

Once you have explained your business situation to the bank officer you can explore the various kinds of special services the bank can offer you to help you get your business off and running.

Helpful Options a Bank May Offer

Protected Checking. Overdraft privileges on personal accounts can extend your cash flow in crunch situations. However, it is easy to absorb this margin into your monthly budget and then the reserve is not available when you really need it.

An Unsecured Loan. This is a loan made by a bank without collateral, to persons whom it knows well. The amount is one the bank is sure you can repay.

A Secured Loan. This is a loan made against collateral. Your business equipment, house, or other valuable property or assets are promised against your repayment.

Casual but Assured Coverage. When a business has a good working relationship with a bank and runs into temporary cash-flow problems, the bank will sometimes cover checks for a week or two (or more) if it knows you are simply waiting for assured accounts receivable. You may find, particularly as your business expands, that cash outlay to fill increased work orders outstrips cash income. Banks are understanding of this if you have a long-standing relationship with them.

When You Run Into Trouble

If you have established a good working relationship with your bank before you need a bail-out, you will be in a better position to get help then otherwise. If this is not the case, you still need to act slightly ahead of time. DON'T BOUNCE CHECKS! Don't run to the bank in a panic. If you see trouble coming—and you shouldn't be taken by surprise, if you've been keeping up with your monthly records—talk it over with the banker.

If you feel you can establish a serious and friendly relationship with the bank, it's time to open an account.

Opening a Business Account

As a sole proprietor, it is not necessary for you to have separate checking accounts for business and personal finances. You can put all your money into the same account. Neither the IRS nor your accountant will mind.

However, if you think you will be better able to keep tabs on your money and stick to a budget if you keep personal money separate from business money, then by all means do it. You'll have twice as many ledgers to balance, but it may be worth it. Personally, I found that there was no benefit to having two accounts in the beginning. There wasn't even enough money to keep one account comfortably afloat—dividing it between two would have been ludicrous. Only after about seven years of freelance did I finally earn enough money that I put myself on a personal budget and kept the rest of my money in either savings and/or a business account. I didn't want to have a large balance in my personal account. I was afraid that I'd feel I could spend it! And I needed to keep myself disciplined. So I put a "salary" into my personal account at the beginning of every month. I put a set amount into another account for business expenses such as typing, office supplies, messengers, etc. These accounts are refilled each month from the savings and investments I have set up. But I consider this the ultimate luxury. And believe me, there was no way I could do it for many, many years.

But, if fortune comes your way sooner than it did for me, or if you just like the idea of separate accounts, here are your options: (1) establishing a second "personal" account for business; or (2) establishing an account under an "assumed" name for business.

If you are conducting a business under an assumed name, you must set up a separate account and obtain authorization to sign checks and make deposits for that account. To do this, give your banker the certificate of registration of your company name to keep on file.

For either type of separate business account, you

need to choose a checkbook format that works easily for you. A notebook ledger style is best. You may even want one that records checks on a carbon stub as you write them. You will:

- Deposit all business income into the account.
- Write all business expense checks from that account.
- Write yourself personal expense checks, to be deposited in your personal account, much like a salary.

If you do not have two accounts, your personal spending money is all mixed up with your business income. Therefore, make sure you note which expenses are for business-related activities and clearly identify all deposits by writing in the source and job to which the income pertains. But, however you set up your checking, you must be able to manage a budget. And no external form will guarantee success unless you are committed to making it work.

Insuring Success

When starting any freelance entrepreneurship, there are certain insurance burdens, both personal and business, that you incur. Additionally, certain special businesses need even more elaborate protection. Some insurance, such as a pension plan, is available through all banks; Savings and Loans also provide life insurance.

Personal Insurance

When you become your own boss, you are no longer protected as under your previous company's insurance plan. You have to make special arrangements to transfer your coverage to an individual policy. Health care, social security, and personal life insurance and pension are your obligations now. Don't forego health insur-

ance! If you do, a sprained ankle or a minor operation
can wipe you out. I know insurance is expensive, but
you aren't really ready to run your own business if
you can't take on this essential financial expense.

Health Care. Although you can take out Blue Cross/
Blue Shield or some comparable plan as an unaffiliated
individual, many freelancers qualify for group plans
with professional associations and groups in their field.
(See blurbs about organizations given in Chapter 10
for information.) Some freelancers, such as musicians,
are union members and can qualify for health care that
way. Others, like writers, may find that their agent's
company has a plan that they can join; a photographer
may become part of a guild plan. Speak to trade and
professional associations in your field to get leads on
this. Your costs are usually somewhat lower than you
would pay under individual coverage and you often get
special coverage—dental care, for example—that you
could not afford on your own.

Life Insurance. Most young people without families
do not have life insurance. But if you have a business
partnership, both partners may want to take out pol-
icies naming each other as beneficiaries, to assure the
continuity of the business if one partner should die.

Social Security Insurance. As mentioned earlier, you
are responsible for paying the self-employment social
security tax when you file your annual income tax
return. As a sole proprietor, you make full payment.
Incorporated businesses split the payment between
corporate and personal accounts.

Pension Plans

For the unincorporated sole proprietor, there are two
basic pension plans available: the IRA (Individual Retirement Account) and the Keogh Plan. They are both
set up with your bank or any other financial institution.

The Keogh Plan. The Keogh Plan is for self-employed
individuals. Subchapter S individuals also qualify. It

provides that you may invest $15,000 or 15% of your net earned income—whichever is less—into a tax-deferred pension account. It is best to work with an accountant to establish this.

The IRA. The Individual Retirement Account (IRA) is available to all taxpayers. It can also be established in addition to a Keogh Plan. It provides that you may invest up to $2000 of your *earned* income per year in a tax-deferred account.

For both the Keogh and IRA, you pay taxes on the invested money when you begin to pay yourself a pension. The tax rate for older people is lower and your overall income bracket will probably be lower too, so the tax paid is less than if you'd been assessed in the year when you earned the money. You cannot get to this money before you are 59½ without a penalty, so think realistically about your overall financial plan. Yet, keep in mind that interest or other income compounding tax free in an IRA doubles much more rapidly than taxed income. You end up with a lot more in dollars.

Simplified Employee Pension. For those of you who have a corporation, and are employed by your corporation, you may combine your IRA and corporate retirement plan in a Simplified Employee Pension (SEP). This allows the corporation *and* the individual to make a contribution to the plan. The money contributed by the corporation can be $15,000 or 15% of an employee's salary, whichever is less. As the employee you can contribute up to $2,000 yourself. Consult your accountant for all the particulars.

Unemployment Insurance

You can pay for your own unemployment protection—in fact, if you're a corporation, you must. This allows you to file for compensation if you lay yourself off because of lack of work! Investigate this with your accountant.

Business Insurance

To protect your businesses from suits and to protect your basic investments and equipment, you can take out various forms of insurance, as described below.

Property Insurance. Fire and theft can destroy even the smallest business. If you've invested all your available cash in office equipment, for example, a home burglary could put an end to your work. Furniture, inventory, and equipment should all be protected. If your business depends on expensive equipment such as cameras or word processors, get insurance immediately.

Liability Insurance. Anytime you have the public coming into your place of business, you need liability protection. If someone trips or hurts himself in any way, you could be sued.

Product Liability. This may apply if you are producing goods or products. If a customer is injured by your product, you may be liable. Discuss this with your attorney or insurance agent.

The rule of thumb here is, if you can't afford the business insurance you need, than you can't afford to be in business.

8 Negotiations and Client Relationships

"Hey, back up a minute. I don't believe what I'm hearing. You, my esteemed client, are refusing to pay me my expenses! Tell me I'm dreaming. Tell me something is wrong with my ears. But don't tell me that again!"

Sam stood up, strode over to where Miss Braithwaite was sitting, and cracked his knuckles about four inches from her pretty face. He'd been a sucker for that face since the first time they'd met. It was a sunny winter morning. He remembered because the light had hurt his eyes so much. He'd been glad to see some potential cash walk in the door. Saunter in, really. She'd seemed sweet and vulnerable. They'd talked casually. He was sure he'd mentioned that his day rate didn't include expenses. But his head had been hurting pretty badly and there wasn't anything on paper to prove what they'd set as terms.

"Let's start over again, like we just met, and see if we can't come to a mutual understanding," Sam *suggested. But in his heart he knew he was a day late and a dollar short one more time.*

Like Sam, we all tend to try and relax a bit after we get the business off the ground. That is a big mistake. Once a business is really off the ground, there are two areas that demand our constant attention: negotiation and maintenance of client relationships. They are intertwined, for if we mess up on either one, it makes it difficult to keep the business going. Blow a negotiation and you've got no cash to flow; squander your cash and you're at a disadvantage in negotiations; fail to keep good client relationships and both negotiations and cash suffer. So, let's look at each process and see how to maximize your business potential.

Negotiations

Any time we reach an agreement with a business client, we have participated in the process of negotiation. Failure to recognize this puts you at a severe disadvantage. For unless you are conscious of the process of striking a deal, you do not have control and can end up agreeing to terms that are less than favorable to your business. (Remember, *you* are your business. If the deal hurts business, it hurts you personally: your creative energy is dampened; your productivity threatened.)

"I was raised to be a businessman," says Steven K. "Funny, but in my own way I turned out to be one. I mean, I run a clown business!"

Steven started doing entertainment at children's parties four years ago. Today he has three other freelance clowns working for him. His company, Clowning Around, is in constant demand.

"I never thought I'd need to know how to make business deals. Everything I did was designed to take me away from that. But it turned out that to do what I want and make a living at it, I need to think pin-stripe underneath the clown suit."

The basic principle of negotiation is that both sides must win!

This is not as improbable as it seems, or as idealistic. You want to achieve parity and cooperation with your clients; they want to get the best work out of you.

When only one negotiator emerges as a winner, both sides lose.

In any negotiation, there are some basic requirements:

1. Know your facts.
2. Listen carefully.
3. Know when you can afford to compromise and when you can not.
4. State your positions simply and clearly.

You must know what it takes to do your job: the time, money, and effort you will have to put out.

You must know the minimal amount of compensation you can receive that will cover those expenditures.

You must have an idea of the grades of work you can perform for the money received. A caterer can provide a simple buffet for twelve, given one budget; a gourmet feast, given another. Likewise, a graphic designer can offer simple solutions to a client's needs with one budget, or provide elegant design and execution on an expanded budget. You must know what your expenses will be.

Furthermore, as you negotiate with a client, you must listen carefully for verbal and nonverbal clues that reveal the client's expectations and desires. Clients are often not familiar with the exact process you must go through to give them what they want. They may not even be sure of what it is they *do* want! Therefore you must tune in and understand their needs, explain them, and show the client what you will do to achieve those results. You can control, in part, the final definition of your job, if you shape the client's ideas during negotiation.

These principles apply to any negotiating situation. However, there are several basic bargaining situations you may encounter. Each one has its own special requirements. Let's look at them and see how they might be handled.

Negotiating in Nonnegotiable Situations

Freelance writers, photographers, illustrators, and the like often work for publications that have set rates. Size or length of the printed work determines the money received—you can take it or leave it. What flexibility is there?

Let's look at the case of a photographer assigned to take two portraits of people featured in a magazine article.

1. The editor calls. You have been trying to get work with him. This is your first assignment.

2. On the phone you are told: the assignment; the technical size requirements of the photos; the location where the photos are to be shot; the delivery date; the use; the money available: "We pay around $150 per shot."

3. You must respond immediately. You calculate the time involved. A half-day? A full day? Two hours? You calculate the expense. Film, processing. Is an assistant needed?

   "I think I can do it in a half-day if the two people come to my studio. My half-day rate is $300, plus expenses. If I have to go to them, however, I will need an assistant. Then I'll have to charge by the hour. I figure it's about a five-hour job with travel and setup, at $100 an hour. I'll provide you with contact sheets of 40 shots each for you to choose from, although I'd like to have some input in the selection process."

4. The editor responds. "It sounds like it's going to be too much money for us. We don't pay more than $150 a shot, expenses included."

5. What flexibility do you have? You can cut quality *or* increase the work load.

   "I'd really like to work with you on these. If you don't care about getting studio-quality portraits, I can shoot them at their offices with available light and a flash—just me and my camera. But you'll have a news-style picture. How will it print and what will the two clients think? The other possibility is that they can come to the

studio for the half-day; perhaps you have another
picture you need for the next issue too. We can
do a 2-for-1 deal. I'll take my chance on my time
and you'll get a bonus. What do you say?"
6. "Is that with or without expenses?"
7. "Expenses are always billed separately."
8. "Okay, let me check. I'll get back to you."

In this situation you must be flexible and accom-
modating (if you want the job), without taking work
that costs you money. Therefore you look for two ways
to satisfy both yourself and your client. In a first-time
situation with a client, the client is testing you. He or
she wants to see how you perform. But if you act like
too much of a contortionist, the client will always expect you to bend over backwards to please him or her—
and that can be a pain!
   Other possible areas of negotiation in a nonnegotiable situation are:

• Credit—do you get a byline or photo credit printed?
• Commitment to future work—do they indicate that
  this is part of a package?
• Retention of ownership of published work—who
  has it?

Handling Verbal Agreements

In many freelance fields, verbal agreements are the
rule of thumb. Whether you work with individuals,
companies or corporations, most arrangements are
made without standard contracts or lawyers or formal
written documents.
   If you run a typing service, for example, your client
brings you a 20-page report to type. You tell her you
charge $2.00 a page. She asks for it in two days. You
nod agreement and she leaves. But lo and behold, when
you start to type, you find that it's hard to read, the
spelling and punctuation are dreadful, and you have to
spend time deciphering it before you can even begin
to type. Furthermore, on your typewriter, with proper
margins, it's going to come out to 26 pages. That will

make the job $12 more than the client expected. What can you do?

Probably this is a lesson that you'll only have to learn once. In this particular situation, you call the client and explain the situation before you continue with the job: "I'm having to spend a lot of time sorting through the pages. This keeps me from typing. I charge $7.50 an hour for this work. It is also turning out longer than your version. I just wanted you to be aware that it will cost you more than $40.00 for this job. Do you want me to continue?"

In all future work, you will lay out these conditions from the start. That way you are not bound by the client's notion of what you will earn.

There is a second type of verbal arrangement that is likely to come up for some freelancers. This involves jobs that are somewhat more complex and are done less immediately. When negotiations have been concluded, you have the time to write a *confirmation letter*. This is not a contract, but a recap of your conversation. It contains a summary of the work to be done, its delivery date, your financial responsibilities, the way expenses will be handled, and the amount of compensation you have agreed to charge. It ends with a paragraph stating: "If these terms are agreeable to you, please give me a call. If not, please note the changes you'd like to make on the letter and return it to me by the beginning of next week. I look forward to working with you." Always keep a copy of this letter in your files!

Drawing Up Your Own Contract Form

Many businesses have standard contractual forms that can be filled out and signed by the freelancer and client at the conclusion of negotiations. Trade and professional organizations can often provide samples. These don't require legal help or the use of an outside negotiator, such as an agent.

To design your own contract, write out two lists: (1) the potential services you will perform for your clients, and (2) the costs for which the clients will be liable.

From these, you can generate the contract. It must be general enough to apply to *all* situations, yet have room for the additions of specific jobs.

A Sample Catering Contract

A Bountiful Buffet, 4723 Skyway Drive, Oak Lake, Ill. 60601

A BOUNTIFUL BUFFET has been hired by _____ to prepare a meal for _____ persons at _____ P.M., _____ (DATE).

MENU: _____
_____
_____

Cost for food: $_____ .

Additionally, THE BOUNTIFUL BUFFET will provide _____ serving helpers @ _____ apiece for an _____ hour shift. Overtime rate is _____ .

Services to be performed by the service personnel: _____
_____

Schedule:
Arrive at clients: _____ .
Set up buffet: _____ .
Serve food: _____ .

Serving dishes and glasses are to be rented by us. The cost is billed directly to you. Beverages and flowers are the client's responsibility.

TOTAL: Price for menu, setup, and service . . . . $_____ .

We reserve the right to make minor changes in the ingredients, depending on the seasonal availability of some foods.

After _____ (DATE), client must pay cancellation fee equal to 50% of total contract. Any increase in number of servings will require an increase in menu charge.

Signed: _____ _____
          THE BOUNTIFUL BUFFET   Date

Signed: _____ _____
                Client   Date

Negotiations Using an Agent or Lawyer

Many freelancers have agents or lawyers who handle their negotiations and deal with the clients on matters of business. These people should be your trusted allies.

To make sure that they represent you with a "voice" that reflects your own, you must go through a process of negotiation with them. You want to use their expertise and advice, but you don't want to abdicate your responsibilities entirely. Tell your agent:

1. How much money you would like for the job and what your minimum is.
2. Explain your expenses and determine how you want them paid for—from your fee, or billed directly to the client.
3. Explain your client relationship to the agent. Is it friendly? Has it been difficult in the past? What is the personality of the client? Prepare your agent.
4. Inform the agent of the length of time you need to do a job well.
5. Determine ahead of time if the agent has the right to refuse work for you without asking you. This is vital.

Furthermore, set up your financial relationship with your agent clearly. Most professions have standard rates for reps, agents, and lawyers. There are percentages of your fee in the case of reps and agents, and flat fees or percentages with lawyers. (Lawyers may also require retainers before the negotiations.) Determine *exactly* what the agent will do for you. How much time will he or she spend trying to secure work for you? Does the agent have good contacts in your field? What is the agent's track record? Who else does he or she represent? Interview him or her. Size the agent up! The agent may be doing you a big favor by taking you on (he or she often would like you to think so, at least), but remember, you pay the agent. You are the one who makes the money for this person!

These are the basic types of negotiations you will encounter. Let's look at them from a slightly different angle, for freelancers will be dealing with clients as diverse as ITT, the local dry cleaners, and the mother of the bride! There are negotiations with: individuals; small business; and corporations. Each one has a different tone.

A freelancer who deals with corporations as a consultant provides a service (weekly flower arrangements, cleaning services, public relations) must contend both with the personality of the corporation and the personality of the individual with whom he or she negotiates. It is important to research the corporate personality. You need to know how adventurous or conservative it is, what the bureaucratic maze is, how hiring is done. Your presentation of yourself, your potential income, and the way you execute the job all depend on reading the corporate style accurately. You can investigate this by reading through the corporation's annual reports, checking out news stories on it, and talking to people who have firsthand knowledge.

If you are acting as a business consultant, you will already know a lot about it, for you are an expert in the field; that's why they're hiring you. But for any clues, the best source of advice to consultants is the Consultant's Library, a division of Bermont Books, Inc., Suite 1108, 815 15th Street, N.W., Washington, D.C., 20005. They have extensive books on negotiating consultant contracts and developing a secure business base.

Writing a Proposal

Whether you are a service freelancer or a consultant for a corporation, you are likely to have to write a proposal before you begin actual verbal negotiations. This is your most important sales pitch—it sets your level of professionalism out in black and white. It can make or break your future business relationships. A proposal contains six basic parts:

1. An explanation of your service, derived from your basic business definition.
2. What it can do for your client.
3. The objective (for both you and your client). What

     you can improve, accomplish, or execute.
4. How you would carry it out.
5. A listing of the specific types of work you handle.
6. Your credentials.

Your proposal may be in two forms:

1. It can be a printed package in a presentation folder: one sheet introduces you and your service. Listings of other clients, experience, and credentials go here.

   Another sheet sets out your pitch to this specific client.

   A final sheet lists basic rates. (This is done only when you do not negotiate your basic prices.)
2. It may be an informal letter of introduction. (This is appropriate when the money involved is not great and the service is not a part of the corporate machinery.)

In either case, the proposal must be completely professional. It should be perfectly typed or printed on fine stationery with a look of substance and success.

Negotiations with Smaller Clients

When you service small businesses or individuals, you want to assure them that you can deliver top-quality work. But beware! They probably are not prepared to pay top money. This is just the simple truth. Whether you're doing an ad for the local market or painting a house for a family down the street, you must do a lot of hand-holding and reassuring. Your job is 50% client relations in a very immediate way.

Such clients rarely have a fixed budget. They just know they want to spend as little as possible. They may ask you to skimp on materials or cut corners in other ways. This can be difficult because such compromises could lower the quality of your work. And that can hurt your reputation, even if it's not your fault. There are no hard-and-fast rules about this, but you must weight the pros and cons carefully.

Maintaining Client Relations

All freelance businesses are built on good client relationships. After negotiations for one job have been completed, even before you have finished your assignment, you must be thinking about getting the next job from a client. You can't succeed without repeat business. The basic rules of client relations are:

1. *Always remember it is business!* These people are not friends, but colleagues.
2. *Speak up.* Say what you want, need, expect, and think from the beginning. Don't be abrasive. Just be open and frank.
3. *Keep in touch.* While a job is going on, check in once a week to let them know you're still out there working. Don't call too often; don't ask them for constant reassurance or advice. Offer them a professional update.
4. *Inform them of problems when appropriate.* A client shouldn't know about the day-to-day hassles you encounter. You're paid to deal with that. But if something comes up that will alter the schedule or change the work—and it's beyond your control or remedy—inform them.
5. *Do a year-round job of P.R.* Send out business Christmas cards. Mail new brochures explaining changes in your services and updating your client references.
6. *Be warm and friendly.* Even though this is a business relationship, not a friendship, it is essential that you show grace and courtesy at all times. Be interested in the other person. Take the time to ask him how he is. Let him enjoy working with you. You will find that you are judged as much on your manner as on your product. People rehire those they get along with. Unless you're a certified genius, you can't expect difficult behavior to be tolerated.
7. *Meet all deadlines.* If you want to be taken seriously, you must deliver *what* you promise *when*

you promise. It sounds simple, but it is not. Work on it.

As you can see, running a freelance business involves two full-time jobs: doing the actual work and dealing with clients. If you can juggle both demands, you will find your enterprise will grow and grow. Then what do you do?

9 The Perils of Success

*The smell of expensive cigar smoke drifted through
the room. There was a hush of success—so different
from the silence of struggle that had filled Sam's
office for the last couple of years. Sally's typewriter
hummed in the front room. A muffled conversation
floated in from the reception area. Sam breathed
deeply and exhaled another plume of Havana fog
across his desk toward the new client he was inter-
viewing. This was getting to be fun. Too bad he
didn't have the energy to really enjoy it. Maybe he'd
just cash it in for awhile. Take a vacation. Relax.
He deserved it.*

*"So what is your fee?" His client's voice brought
him back to the matter at hand.*

*(My fee? Oh, what can I get away with? What
will scare him off? I gotta get a lot for this. And
even then, how am I going to have the time to do
it all myself?)*

*"Well," he began, "an organization like mine
provides very special services to clients such as you.
Of course premium service does imply premium
rates...." Behind his back, he crossed his fingers
and hoped the phone would ring before he had to
come up with the final figure.*

Success kills off as many businesses as failure! How?
By causing you to overextend yourself financially *and*
physically.

Once you have a steady flow of ever-increasing work,

you reach a threshold. There is no more time in the day to earn money. You cannot increase your income, experience, or scope without making changes. The following list describes some problems success may bring; later we'll discuss some solutions.

1. *You will have to turn down some jobs.* What a joy! But how do you make the selections? How do you drop old clients gracefully? How can you be sure new clients are really in your best interest?

2. *Your rates must be raised.* It's time for a raise. But what will the market bear? How much more money do you need to earn? How do you pass along increases to old clients?

3. *You may need to hire help.* Even if you pick your jobs and increase your rates, you may have more work than you can handle. What kind of help do you need? Where can you find it? How do you pick the right person? Can you afford it? Do you know how to delegate authority and how to be a boss?

4. *You may need to make capital investments.* Suddenly your original equipment is not good enough to handle the increasing volume of work. But Ouch! Can you finance your expansion? Is credit available? What are your investment priorities?

5. *You must change your self-image to fit the expanding business.* Less tangible but just as far-reaching is the psychological effect of success. You are no longer a tucked-away cottage industry. You have more and more responsibilities and pressures. Can you handle them?

These are the major issues facing any business person as he or she enters the second stage. How you handle them determines your financial future and professional status. Let's examine them in detail.

Choosing Work

When it comes time to turn work down, you must be able to decide which clients are best for you. Those who have given you work over the months and years, upon whom your reputation is built, may no longer offer you the opportunities you seek. New clients may or may not offer repeat business. When is it time to make the move into the unknown?

Redefining Client Relationships

The time may come when you must change your relationship with a client of long standing. If it is at all possible, never burn a bridge! Good will is your most valuable asset. Don't alienate old clients. You may need them again to pay the rent. If you are gracious, they will respect you for being successful. It makes you more desirable. It confirms their early judgment that you are a quality operation. So if you find you are faced with the possibility of turning down a job from a client who has come to take you for granted:

- Recommend another person to do the job.
- See if the client can juggle his or her schedule so that you have time to work on the client's job.
- Consider hiring a freelancer to actually do the job—and spend the time—so you act only as supervisor of the work.

Premium Rates. If the client cannot commit to a schedule, then she may accept the imposition of a rush service charge for jobs she brings you on short notice. This encourages her to plan ahead and gives you an interest in keeping her around. The premium can be a set percentage of the total job cost; a flat fee; or a pass-along of added expenses you incur in rush circumstances.

Dissolving an Old Business Relationship. If you don't want to continue with an old client, you can handle the situation in several ways. But always give them as much advance warning as possible. Don't drop the news when they're counting on you. One way to handle the situation is to write a disassociation letter. Express your gratitude for the work the client has given you. Reassure the client that the relationship has been beneficial to you. (So, maybe you lie a little!) Explain the changes in direction that your business is going through. There is no need to justify your decision or go into detail. Simply say, "Due to a shift in our interests and in the marketplace, we are no longer going to be able to do the kind of work you require."

Another way to handle the situation is to meet with the client. In person, express your gratitude and present your reasons for deciding not to continue working for the client. In both cases, leave the back door open, with a statement like: "If your needs shift in the future, please consider calling on me again."

Choosing New Clients

But what do you do if the choice is between two new clients? They are both unknown quantities. They both have their charms. Money alone is not the basis for a sound decision. Although an enormous difference in earnings can be the final factor, there are times when more is less—in the long run. Here are some factors to investigate:

- Consider the potential for repeat business. Who is more likely to use you on a regular basis?
- Consider the reputations of the clients. Which offers a better working situation? Which is a more prestigious client? Which client enhances your credentials?
- Consider the people you will be working with or for. What personality problems are there? Whom do you respect more? Whom can you learn from, too?
- Which job are you more qualified for? Although you want to expand your talents, you don't want to rise to your level of incompetence.

As you can see, this type of situation demands a judgment call. This is where that tuned-in sense of intuition we spoke of earlier comes into play. Work on it. Sharpen your ability to recognize advantageous situations.

Raising Rates

Rates are increased for two reasons: one, to cover expanding overhead; and two, to give you a larger profit or salary—two worthy causes, no doubt. In businesses that have set rates, it can be done more simply than in those that require individual negotiations for each job. But whatever the situation, there are certain guidelines to consider.

Cost of Business and Living Increases

Calculating Increased Business Overhead. Returning to your Preliminary Business Plan, compare the figures you logged as fixed costs with your current costs. Have rent, phone, and electricity gone up? What is the percentage of the increase? *Business overhead* is increased by the percentage of increase of your basic rent deduction. If 20% of your rent is considered a business expense, then 20% of any rent increase is an elevation of your business overhead. (Remember, your personal expenses come out of your "salary.")

Enter the current business overhead costs in your revised business plan. The difference between your initial monthly overhead and your current monthly overhead gives you the first figure in determining how much you need to raise your rates.

Calculating Increased General Business Expenses. Have your nonbillable general office expenses increased? Look through your monthly account ledger and compare totals over the last six months. Are you spending more and more on supplies and general maintenance? Approximate the average monthly increase. This amount provides you with the second figure you need to determine how much more money you must earn every month just to stay even!

Calculating Increased Personal Overhead. Finally, this is where your profit comes in—almost. For any basic increase in rates must cover your increased personal overhead first. How much of an increase has there been in the percentage of the rent, phone, and electricity that comes out of your pocket? Have your other personal expenses increased? Calculate them carefully. If possible, prorate them to a monthly figure.

Add the three figures together:

> Increased monthly business overhead: _____
> \+ increased monthly business expenses: _____
> \+ increased monthly personal expenses: _____
> TOTAL: _____

The total is the minimum amount by which you must raise your monthly income in order to stay even.

Settling for a Cost-of-Living Raise

Given the volume of work you take in in a month, how much more must each job generate? If you earn your money in three, six, or more, monthly installments, simply multiply the figures by that time period.

Sometimes it is not possible to raise your rates more than the minimum amount you require. You can gauge your clients' responses and judge what the market will bear. If so, at least you are not losing money. There is no sin in staying even, in this day and age.

The rule of thumb here: check overhead costs every six months and make adjustments!

Cost of Services or Product Increases

Once you have nudged your rates upward to cover your basic expenses, it is time to consider raising the cost of your services. Initially you priced yourself so that you were competitive but also price-desirable. Now it's time to elevate your status and perhaps change your market.

When you revise your scale, you must contend with three issues:

- Old clients' reactions to paying more for the same work.
- The necessity of upgrading your product or service to a level that justifies your rates.
- The possibility that higher rates place you in a new market.

Let's see how to negotiate these problems and explore ways of notifying your clients of the rate changes.

Notifying Old Clients About Rate Increases

When your rate increase is going to affect clients who have grown accustomed to paying you a fixed amount for your services, you must notify them in a professional manner.

There are two distinct freelance situations: the negotiated and the posted-rate businesses. If you operate on a job-by-job process of negotiation, each client will be subject to an individual increase. Writers, for example, who have a minimum standard of, say, $100 per published page, may be paid $115 by one magazine and $125 by another. They must decide if they want to raise only the $115 rate (to $125), or if they want a 10% increase across the board.

Some freelancers, such as photographers, use a combination of a fixed day rate and individual negotiations. One New York freelancer started out notifying ad agencies that he charged $400 per day. When he upped his rate to $750, his entire business shifted. Previously, he had been considered for agency jobs that paid $400 or less. No one ever offered him an $800-a-day job, nor did they try to get him to do an $800 job for $400. But when he raised his rate, he was put into another pool. Now he is considered for jobs, in the same agencies, that bill between $750–$1,000 a day! True, he doesn't get any of those little jobs now. But who needs them?

Freelancers who have posted rates—typing at $2.00 a page, childcare at $4.50 an hour, housecleaning at $35 a day, crocheted sweaters at $60 apiece—don't have to deal with individual clients. The freelancer may simply make an across-the-board announcement, through promotional mailings or in person.

Whatever your situation, follow these guidelines:

- Give old clients advance warning. At the completion of a job, notify them that the next one will cost more.
- Tie the increase into an increase in the kinds of service you will provide or an increase in quality or quantity of your product line.
- Allow clients to meet the increase in steps. If you are going for a 20% rate increase, spread it out. Increase their costs 6.66% on the next three jobs.

Upgrading Your Service

As your rates climb, you may need to expand your scope or the quality of your service. If you run a typing service, perhaps you can add a free pickup or proofreading service to justify your higher costs. A caterer may change the type of menus or offer table-decorating services to justify his price-worthiness.

In any business, expansion of rates should reflect increases in professionalism, quality, and service. But don't offer new services that take money out of one pocket while you're trying to put it in the other!

Changing Markets

As your business grows, you will learn which market offers you the most work. You may have targeted your clothes-buying service to wealthy customers when you conceived your preliminary business plan. But time has shown you that middle-income working women are your greatest source of income. It's time to reshape your promotional efforts and explore new department-store connections to take advantage of this emerging pool of potential clients.

This learn-as-you-do experience affects every type of freelance business, so all of you should return to the PBP and go through the research, promotion, and targeting steps again. Constantly hone your self-promotion skills.

- Target new sources of clients.
- Produce new promotional mailings.
- Set up new interviews and connections.

Business is an organic system that must grow and change to adapt to its ever-changing environment. Your responsiveness and attention to these shifts can make the difference between failure and long-term survival.

Determining the Amount of a Rate Increase

When it comes time to actually make the rate increase, you must determine what the market will bear *and* what you need to earn.

- Check out the competition. Always keep tabs on what others are charging.
- Investigate those who charge more than you. Do they offer more services? Do they have more experience? Do they reach a different market?
- Identify what makes your business better than the competition. List your assets. What is special about you?
- Determine how much more money you need to earn per month or per year. Once you have arrived at an annual figure, determine how much more per job (based on the volume of work you now have) you must charge. This figure is a "guesstimate." Now, how much more than that do you feel you can charge and still be attractive to your potential clients? Guard against grandiosity!
- Once you have determined a figure, test the waters. If you find after a month or so that the rates are keeping you from getting new work, you'll have to scale them down again.

Hiring Help

Expansion often means that you need extra help to get your work done. If you are spending too much time on the everyday tasks of keeping the office going, you are cutting into your ability to generate work and practice your talents. If you've taken on more and more complex jobs, you may need an assistant or colleague to work alongside you. In either case, you must know how to find the right person and how it affects your financial stability. Here are some suggestions:

- Always hire other freelancers. Do not put anyone "on the books." It is too much overhead!
- Use part-time help.
- Consider hiring assistants on a commission basis.
- Know precisely what you want your employee to do. Don't waste time or money.

Michael M. was a junior high school teacher in the Chicago public schools when he began running a charter travel service during his summers off.

"I think I wasn't really running a freelance business until about five years ago," he says. "And now I run a full-scale small business. I can't tell you exactly what the difference is, but it has something to do with size and seriousness—to me at least."

"I love travel. If I could do it all the time, I'd love it. When I started, my motive was to get free airfare for myself and make some extra money. So I began organizing charters for teachers. That went on for several years, first during summer months, then gradually during other school holidays. I quit teaching five years ago."

The transition was not easy. Charters fell through, travelers were disgruntled. "Weather, political events, anything can mess you up. And I was so used to the steady income from teaching. It scared me to death." He thinks a minute. "Well, really it scared me to life. I had to keep going to survive. Now I've got two employees. That's the difference between just playing around and really running a business. I am completely committed and my employees depend on me."

Determining Your Needs

What kind of help do you need?

Survey your business. Where are the bottlenecks? Are letters unanswered, phone calls unreturned? Is your filing system in chaos? Are you keeping up your books? Do you need someone to make client contact? Or a rep to take around your work? Would someone who is talented in the same areas you are be able to do some of the less creative tasks like proposal-writing, job preparation, or research?

List your trouble spots. Describe the type of employee who could handle those tasks.

Getting More Than You Pay For

What you really want, in a typist or a co-worker, is someone who is as talented, hard-working, bright, and responsible as you! But you don't want to pay the person for it! You're looking for someone who's overqualified but content to be in a learning position.

- Pick people who plan to move on to better jobs. You may lose them sooner than you'd like, but while they are with you, they'll give you a lot of help.
- Pick people who realize that they can learn from you. This assures you that they will feel there is a purpose for taking a low-paying job.
- Offer employees a chance to expand their responsibilities. If a secretary shows initiative, encourage it.
- Train them to do more and more. You must show patience and guidance.
- Go on your intuition. Sometimes the most qualified person (on paper) is not the best-suited. You must judge personality and character.
- Set up a few unbendable rules. Hours are to be

strictly observed. When necessary, proper dress should be a requirement. Within these parameters, allow freedom of style.

If you choose wisely and offer an environment that is businesslike but easygoing, you will find you can keep an overqualified employee content and loyal for longer than you might imagine.

What Can You Afford?

Any increase in overhead must be justified by the increase in income it generates. The expense of hiring office help must be offset by your increased ability to hustle more work and do more on the jobs you have. If you hire a co-worker to take on actual jobs, which you supervise, then the expense must be covered by the income on that job *and* there must still be enough to give you a cut. It must also cover the intangible expenses incurred by having to provide work space and supplies (and even food) for a second person. For example, if a co-worker can do a $1,200 job while you are doing a $2,000 one, it appears superficially that that should help the business. But, let's look at the figures closely:

- You pay the co-worker a flat fee of $250 per week.
- The job takes three weeks (3 × $250 = $750 in salary).
- You spend $150 to set up the co-worker's work area.
- You feed him lunch for 15 days × $4.00 a day ($60.00).
- The cost to you = $960.
- Your profit = $1,200 - $960, or $240.

Is an increased income of $240 for three weeks' time (or $80 per week) enough to compensate you for the hassles and responsibilities you've taken on? Only you can judge. How much do you need the money? What are the positive, intangible results of having your business handle a higher volume? Does it enhance your prestige? Your visability? Your contacts?

In either situation, whether your gains are financial or intangible from having a helper, you do gain a tax deduction. The freelancer's salary is a business expense. Ask your accountant to calculate the possible gain.

Tax Note: Any freelance employee who earns more than $600 in one year from you must receive a 1099-NEC Form from you before tax time, Statement for Recipients of Nonemployee Compensation. You submit a copy with your tax return and your employee is responsible for declaring the income on his or her tax return, too. You need invoices from these assistants for their work, for tax purposes.

Being a Boss

When you hire an employee you become that person's boss! For many entrepreneurs, this is not an easy role. It means you must both assume authority and delegate responsibility. The following are some suggestions to keep the employer-employee relationship running well:

- Make your expectations clear; define the job precisely.
- Provide a comfortable work environment.
- Pay promptly.
- Don't butt in all the time; keep a watchful but distant eye. Allow for small mistakes, but try to anticipate large ones.
- Don't let irritations build. You are the boss. If you have a complaint, express it—politely. Don't be afraid of your authority. Otherwise, you find yourself in the position of the people who always clean the house before the cleaning person comes so that the cleaner won't think they are slobs or feel overworked.

Making Capital Investments

As your business grows, your original equipment may become worn out or outdated. To rise to new levels of success, you may have to invest money in new equipment on the chance that it will ultimately generate more work. This is a tricky decision. Occasionally you can make a capital purchase coincide with a specific job that pays for it—but that's rare.

Determine Priorities

- List what you would purchase—in the best of all worlds.
- Investigate the best sources for the equipment.
- Enter prices in your priorities list.
- Determine which items you have cash on hand to purchase.
- Which items can be bought on credit from the source?
- What are the terms?
- Which items require a loan from a bank or credit union? Speak with your banker to see if financing is a realistic possibility.

Now, balancing need, price, money available, and credit, which piece of equipment is your:

> First choice_____
> Second choice_____
> Third choice_____

Calculate the Effect on Cash Flow

Go to your monthly P&L and cash-flow ledgers. Determine how the expenditure will affect your financial stability.

Find Work to Offset Expense

If, for example, you want to purchase a color developing and printing system for your darkroom, begin to develop clients for that service now! Send out flyers to all old clients, announcing the upcoming new service. Target new clients who may need the service. Make contacts. Generate interest and potential work. This will allow you to recoup your investment as soon as possible after purchasing the new equipment.

As you can see, expansion demands that you deal with many tough issues—turning down work, hiring help, increasing your rates, and making investments. All are related. One may trigger the next. There is no clear-cut order to them; you must be alert to each one. This pressure adds to the most common danger faced by freelancers entering the second stage: burnout.

Burnout

You have worked day and night for several years. Vacations have been few and far between. It seems you have either the money or the time, but never both together! The pressure begins to erode your stamina. You are overly upset by small setbacks. Even the joy of success isn't enough to keep you enthusiastic. Tahiti looks very inviting—as a permanent place to live. A job in a company, a regular salary, is appealing. You've begun to feel like a drudge.

There are few simple cures for this creeping disease. But when all else fails, try the following:

- Begin to schedule in "rest periods" in every week. Schedule your fun. Make yourself take off Tuesday afternoons. Join an exercise class, play tennis regularly, or do one thing you love, just for yourself every week.
- Reexamine how you spend your time. If you've been working twelve hours a day for a couple of years, you're a workaholic. It is a habit. Do you really use that time well? Can you accomplish as much in fewer hours if you are more organized?
- Are you still terrified of failure? Is it a realistic

fear? Assess your status. Give yourself credit. Take pleasure and pride in your accomplishments. Focus on your achievements, not your potential mistakes.

- Take a break. If you can afford it, take a month off. You are in control of your schedule. Arrange future jobs so you can rest, knowing you have work when you get back to your desk.
- Just imagine what you'd really feel like having to go into an office every day. Come on—you know it would be terrible. No more walks in the midday sun, no more being your own boss; having to deal with office politics. Yuk! Remember why you went freelance in the first place? Give yourself a pep talk.

When you feel weary or afraid, just remember you are in good company. You've turned a dream into a business. You are one of the fortunate few who has reached the second stage.

"Ideas are a dime a dozen. That's why a huge percentage of all small businesses fail. It takes more than an idea to make a go of it. An entrepreneurial business requires someone who can take an idea and translate it into action."

When William Schmick speaks, people listen. As an investment sales broker, founder and motivating force behind New York University's Entrepreneurial Exchange, and head of five thriving small businesses dealing with everything from real estate to computer software, he is a certified expert.

"The crucial elements in any entrepreneurial manager are management skills, a willingness to spend a lot of time on the job, and a rapport with people," Schmick notes. "Luckily, these skills are learnable. I learned them. The hard way. Maybe the only way. I was willing to fail and rebound until I got it right."

Like so many of the other successful freelancers I interviewed, Schmick personifies an essential truth. In freelance, success is not determined so much by how you handle good fortune, but how you handle failure.

You need the ability to rebound, to keep fighting, to get over the inertia caused by disappointment or fatigue. Only then can you enjoy the rewards of the success.

10 Resources

If you've gotten this far, you qualify as an entrepreneur! The freelance life, when handled right, is a privilege and a pleasure. The sense of accomplishment is highly rewarding. You test yourself over and over in many ways and develop skills and abilities you may never have known you had.

But there are no promises, no sure bets. The business may not sustain you forever. What *will* sustain you is your energy, your drive. You must be able to fail and then rebound by moving on to the next incarnation of your business dream.

There are an infinite number of possible freelance entrepreneurships. The limit is your imagination and talent. And those can be expanded, far more than you may think.

To help you understand the scope of possibilities and show where you can go for advice and guidance, I included the following detailed listing of source material: first, a look at the general business advice available; then, a survey of the specialized services available to a wide range of particular freelance occupations.

1. General Business Advice and Information Resources

U. S. Department of Commerce
Bureau of the Census
Public Information Office
Washington, D.C. 20233
(202) 763–4040

The Census Bureau publishes an enormous number of pamphlets on business. Call them and ask for guidance and a copy of their publications list.

Small Business Administration
1441 L Street N.W.
Washington, D.C. 20416
(202) 653–6365

A major resource for information and advice, the SBA offers published bibliographies on everything from managing a handicrafts business to dealing with banks. They have a publications list outlining their free pamphlets *and* their modestly priced books. Do not overlook this source. whatever your business or your questions.

SCORE
1129 20th Street N.W.
Suite 410
Washington, D.C. 20416
(202) 653–6279

This organization, sponsored by the SBA, offers owners of small businesses the advice and counsel of retired executives. They can help you identify problems and find solutions to all your management questions. If you want to join, write the national headquarters or contact your local chapter and a counselor will get in touch with you.

New York University Entrepreneurs Exchange
N.Y.U. Graduate School of Business
100 Trinity Place
New York, N.Y. 10006
(212) 285–6000

This exchange puts MBA candidates together with business persons who need advice and improved management techniques. The Entrepreneurs Exchange was developed

to help the graduate student learn what it's really like to
run a business and to give entrepreneurs access to help
from well-trained future business managers.

Encyclopedia of Associations '83 (17th edition)
Published by Gale Research Co.,
Book Tower,
Detroit, Mich. 48226
Editor: Denise S. Akey
(313) 961–2242

This compendium of all trade and professional associations can lead you to the group that specializes in your
specific area of business. These associations are not, however, universally useful. Some are strictly for profit, some
have a slightly fanatic edge, some are the result of a particular obsession or political perspective. However, careful reading of the entries and a phone call, plus a reading
of their literature, should let you decide if any group is
really going to fit your needs or not. When they are good,
they provide educational programs, support and often such
things as group insurance.

2. Financial Advice

National Foundation for Consumer Credit
8701 Georgia Avenue, Suite 601
Silver Springs, Md. 20910

Offering small businesses debt counseling for a nominal
fee of $10.00 or so, the NFCC can help you when you've
really run into bad money-management problems. (May
you never need them!)

I.R.S. Small Business Tax Workshops

This service, offered through local IRS offices, can help
you prepare your taxes. Contact your local office, or in
New York call (212) 264–3420.

Volunteer Lawyers for the Arts
1560 Broadway, Suite 711
New York, N.Y. 10036
(212) 575–1150

For freelance artists, this volunteer organization offers in-person legal advice plus some valuable publications, including *Fear of Filing*, a guide to taxes and the self-employed.

Businessman's Information Guide
American Institute of Certified Public Accountants
Order Dept.
1211 Avenue of the Americas
New York, N.Y. 10036
(212) 575–6200

Despite the name, the content of this book is invaluable and of use to all freelancers. It covers all accounting systems and offers really clear guidelines on setting up your business.

How to Read a Financial Report
Merrill Lynch Pierce Fenner and Smith, Inc.
25 Broadway
New York, N.Y. 10004
(212) 637–7455

This publication offers a concise guide to understanding the basic structure and function of a financial report and is useful if you should need to write one for an investor or bank.

Tax Guide for Small Business
Department of Treasury
IRS Publication #334

This IRS publication is available through all local offices. It is just one of the many IRS publications that can help you understand tax laws as they pertain to specific businesses.

Bender's Dictionary of 1040 Deductions
Matthew Bender & Co., Inc.
1275 Broadway
Albany, N.Y. 12201

At last a completely readable explanation of every 1040 Form! Deductions, regulations, audit dangers, and a line-by-line explanation of tax forms make this a really useful tool.

3. Advertising Advice

Association of National Advertisers
155 East 44th Street
New York, N.Y. 10017
(212) 697–5950

If you want information on how best to advertise your business, ANA offers information on creative advertising and on placing ads in all forms of media.

Direct-Mail Marketing Association
6 East 43rd Street
New York, N.Y. 10017
(212) 689–4977

If you want to advertise your business through direct-mail marketing outlets, this organization can tell you what your options are.

American Association of Advertising Agencies
666 Third Avenue
New York, N.Y. 10017
(212) 682–2500
(L.A. office: (213) 657–3711

If you are starting up a small advertising business and are looking for advice and information, call or write to this group.

Also see the SBA listing under section 1 of this list to obtain government publications on advertising a small business.

4. Organizations For the Arts

American Council for the Arts
570 Seventh Avenue
New York, N.Y. 10018
(212) 354–6655

Besides providing members with an interesting magazine and newsletter on the status of the arts in America, the ACA publishes a whole roster of books that are of great help to any artist trying to conduct business. Information on grants, contracts, management and organization in the visual arts, graphics, and theater is covered in detail. The ACA also conducts art/business seminars that might be of interest.

Alliance of Resident Theaters of New York
325 Spring Street
New York, N.Y. 10013
(212) 989–5257

Set up to assist those interested in a career in theater, ART has extensive employment information on technical, administrative and design-related jobs in the theatrical field. They also sponsor an intern placement program. This is also a good clearinghouse for graphic artists and painters interested in set design or musicians with a desire to freelance in sound for the theater.

Arts and Business Council
130 East 40th Street
New York, N.Y. 10016
(212) 683–5555

Working with corporations and arts organizations (not usually individuals), this organization provides guidance to groups writing funding and grants proposals. They provide counseling for those trying to conduct an arts organization in a businesslike manner. So even if you are not an "organization" per se, they may provide help or guidance.

Media Alliance
Fort Mason, Building D
San Francisco, Calif. 94123

A nonprofit group sponsoring workshops, classes, and panels on the business of writing, publishing, broadcasting, TV, and photography. Offers legal help, a medical plan, and job file. It is a good social/professional network of national contacts though it's in the Bay Area.

Volunteer Lawyers for the Arts

See listing in "Financial Advice" section of this list (section 2).

●Crafts

American Craft Council
Library
44 West 53rd Street
New York, N.Y. 10019
(212) 397–0638

The Council publishes *American Craft*, a bimonthly magazine, and has resources and services for the artist. Library membership gives you health insurance, magazine, free entry to exhibition openings, information on fairs, suppliers, schools, etc.

International Association of Fairs and Expositions
M.P.O. Box 65801
Springfield, Mo. 65801

Many craftspersons find fairs and expos to be a profitable way to sell their products and gain recognition in diverse geographic areas. If you want to take your craft on the road, IAFE can tell you when, where and how.

Society of North American Goldsmiths
2849 Saint Ann Drive
Green Bay, Wis. 54301

An organization for jewelry designers and craftspersons that has interesting publications and sponsors shows.

Center for the History of American Needlework
Carlow College
3333 Fifth Avenue
Pittsburgh, Pa. 15213

A valuable resource center for information and ideas, this organization is dedicated to keeping the history of textile and needlework design alive. If you are looking for ideas for your product designs, their pattern portfolios and books are very useful.

Creative Cash
by Barbara Brabec
HP Books
Box 5367
Tucson, Ariz. 85703
(602) 888–2150

A basic how-to on selling your crafts, needlework designs, etc. Gives avenues of selling, interviews, inspiration, practical tips.

The Crafts Report
For subscriptions: P.O. Box 1992
Wilmington, Del. 19899
(Editorial offices: 3632 Ashworth North, Seattle, Wash. 98103)

Published eleven times per year, it offers business and marketing advice and information about individual crafts persons. For professionals.

●Photography

American Society of Magazine Photographers
205 Lexington Avenue
New York, N.Y. 10016
(212) 889–9144

Full membership is available to photographers with at least three years' professional journalistic and print experience. For those with less than three years experience, an associate membership is offered. The ASMP provides insurance, advice, and a network of contacts. The cost of membership and procedures for joining vary depending on your status.

Friends of Photography
P.O. Box 500
Sunset Center
Carmel, Calif. 93921
(408) 624–6330

This prestigious organization, with Ansel Adams as its Trustee Chairman, sponsors shows, publishes books, and runs training workshops.

Sell Your Photographs: The Complete Marketing Strategy for the Freelancer
by Natalie Canavor
Madrona Publishers, Inc.
2116 Western Avenue
Seattle, Wash. 98121
(206) 624–6840

How to Make Money with Your Camera
by Ted Schwarz
HP Books
Box 5367
Tucson, Ariz. 85703
(602) 888–2150

●Film and Video

National Academy of Television Arts and Sciences
110 West 57th Street
New York, N.Y. 10019
(212)586–8424

This is the group that conducts the Emmy Awards. They
also hold workshops and seminars on the creative and
business aspects of TV, and have a remarkable film and
tape library for research in the field.

Young Filmakers Foundations
4 Rivington Street
New York, N.Y. 10002
(212) 673–9361

For beginners in film this organization offers training
workshops in film and video and has postproduction facilities available for members' use.

Association of Independent Video and Filmmakers, Inc.
625 Broadway
9th floor
New York, N.Y. 10012
(212) 473–3400

A nonprofit trade association for independent filmmakers,
AIVF provides group medical insurance, seminars, information on grants, production and distribution, and as-
sists with the distribution of short films nationally and
internationally.

●Visual and Graphic Arts

Artists Equity Association
3726 Albemarle Street, N.W.
Washington, D.C. 20016

This professional society of visual artists works to advocate pro-arts legislation. Additionally, they have informational "Action Kits" that address artists' business, management, and professional problems. Write for publications lists.

Graphic Artists Guild
30 East 20th Street
New York, N.Y. 10003
(212) 777–7353

A "union" for graphic artists, the Guild offers a network for any graphic artist across the country. Legal advice, business counsel, and general support are also available.

Art Information Center
280 Broadway
Room 412
New York, N.Y. 10007
(212) 227–0282

A free clearinghouse of information for painters, the Center lists exhibits, where to find various artists' work, and classes. Oriented to helping contemporary living artists, it works with professionals to aid in gallery referrals. Write for information or call. Office visits are by appointment only.

Society of Scribes
P.O. Box 933
New York, N.Y. 10150

A small professional organization for calligraphers, SOS provides workshops and lectures in the New York area and puts you in contact with a network of like-minded scribes.

Independent Signcrafters of America
P.O. Box 605
Marietta, Ohio 45750

For professional signcrafters, this organization offers workshops on various techniques and graphic processes.

Society of Illustrators
128 East 63rd Street
New York, N.Y. 10021
(212) 838–2560

Established in 1901, this is a nonprofit professional and educational organization. The public can take advantage of its art gallery, studio classes, and lecture series. Juried shows are held for students and professionals. The Society offers an artist membership and an associate membership for those associated with the field.

The Graphic Arts Technical Foundation
4615 Forbes Avenue
Pittsburgh, Pa. 15213

Concerned with the newest technology for printing, lithography, and photography, this organization focuses on professional printers who work with large presses. There is, however, information on interesting printing and photo techniques that might interest the smaller scale artist and craftsperson. Their publications catalogue is fascinating. Membership is really only for companies, employees of companies, teachers, and students.

●**Writers**

American Society of Journalists and Authors
1501 Broadway
Suite 1907
New York, N.Y. 10036
(212) 997–0947

A professional organization for freelance nonfiction writers who have a track record, this group also offers beginning writers an annual nonfiction writers' conference. Additionally, regional chapters offer smaller seminars throughout the year. Contact the headquarters for information.

The International Women's Writing Guild

(See entry in section 17, "Women's Reference Sources.")

Washington Independent Writers
525 National Press Building
Washington, D.C. 20045
(202) 347–4973

A trade association for freelance writers, Washington Independent Writers provides its 1,400 members with health insurance, legal services, a job bank, newsletter, and workshops.

The National Writers Club
1450 S. Havana
Suite 620
Aurora, Colo. 80012
(303) 751–7844

Membership is available to established professionals and beginners. Publishes a magazine called *Freelancer's Market* and other pertinent newsletters.

Associated Writing Programs
Old Dominion University
Norfolk, Va. 23508

If you are looking for an academic program in creative writing to help you hone your skills, this organization has an extensive catalogue of such programs.

The Writers Theatre
P.O. Box 810
Times Square Station
New York, N.Y. 10108
(212) 777–7005

A nonprofit organization for poets, novelists, and playwrights designed to help new works and adaptations find theatrical production. Sponsors workshops and readings. They will send you a newsletter outlining their activities.

Profitable Part-Time Full-Time Freelancing—A Step-by-Step Guide to Writing Your Way to Freedom and Financial Success
by Clair F. Rees
Writer's Digest Book Club
9933 Alliance Road
Cincinnati, Ohio 45242
(513) 984–0717

This is a personal account of Mr. Rees' career as a writer, with advice on business and tips on keeping your spirits up.

Author Law & Strategies
by Brad Bunnin and Peter Beren
Nolo Press
950 Parker Street
Berkeley, Calif. 94710

A general guide that outlines legal considerations of writing. It should not take the place of a lawyer or agent, however.

Writer's Digest (magazine)
9933 Alliance Road
Cincinnati, Ohio 45242
(513) 984–0717

This grandfather of writer-advice publications covers "how-to-get-published" advice plus guidance on good commercial form for all types of fiction and nonfiction articles.

Publishers Weekly
R.R. Bowker Company
1180 Avenue of the Americas
New York, N.Y. 10036
(212) 764–5100

P.W. is the book industry weekly. It is a sure-fire way to stay current with trends in book publishing and information on each publishing house.

●Music

National Academy of Popular Music
One Times Square, 8th floor
New York, N.Y. 10036

If you're a musician looking for training, you might investigate the National Academy of Popular Music. They conduct song-writing seminars.

National Association of Composers, U.S.A.
133 West 69th Street
New York, N.Y. 10023

A nonprofit organization, NAC offers information and educational guidance on how to be a professional composer.

Billboard
1515 Broadway
New York, N.Y. 10036
(212) 764–7300

This weekly music business magazine also publishes books relating to the field. Of special interest: *This Business of Music* (4th Ed.); and *More About This Business of Music* (3rd ed.).

●Dance

Dance Theatre Workshop
219 West 19th Street
New York, N.Y. 10011
(212) 691–6500

Set up originally as a choreographers' coop, DTW now offers production facilities, artist sponsorship programs, and a wide variety of preproduction assistance to performing artists throughout the country. Want access to performing in New York? Here's a place to begin. Additionally—poets, mimes, and visual artists can use DTW facilities and support.

American Dance Guild, Inc.
570 Seventh Avenue
New York, N.Y. 10018
(212) 944–0557

For all types of dancers, the ADG offers educational programs and has a placement service for jobs in the dance field.

5. Consulting

Institute of Management Consultants, Inc.
19 West 44th Street
New York, N.Y. 10036
(212) 921–2885

This licensing group certifies consultants with a minimum of 5 years of professional field experience. However, they also are of use to those just starting a management consulting business, because of their publications and seminars.

The Consultants Bookstore
Templeton Road
Fitzwilliam, N.H. 03447

Write to them for their catalogue. They have a good selection of titles.

6. Cooking, Catering

How to Make Money in Your Kitchen
by Jeffrey Feinman
William Morrow & Company, Inc.
105 Madison Avenue
New York, N.Y. 10016
(212) 889–3050

General advice on the different ways to turn cooking skills into money-making business.

Income from Your Own Business: Cater from Your Kitchen
by Marjorie P. Blanchard
Playboy Press Paperbacks
1633 Broadway
New York, N.Y.10019
(212) 688–3030

A basic guide to starting and maintaning a home-based catering service. How to make your kitchen work-ready.

Cashing In On Cooking
by Nancy C. Baker
Contemporary Books, Inc.
180 N. Michigan Avenue
Chicago, Ill. 60601
(312) 782–9181

One more book offering encouragement to those looking to turn a talent into a business.

How to Make Money in Cake Decorating: Owning and Operating
  A Successful Business in Your Home
by Del Carnes
Denver © 1981 Deco Press Pub.
500 E. 84th Avenue
Denver, Colo.
(303) 289–1267

A "how-to" covering the art and business of cake decorating. Tips on getting business apply to all food and catering enterprises.

7. Editorial Services, Typing, Secretarial Work

Independent Professional Typists Network
12 Chicory Way
Irvine, Calif. 92715

For sole proprietors running calligraphic, typing, trans-
lation, record/bookkeeping, or general editorial services,
IPTN offers support and information.

Professional Association of Secretarial Services
2200 E. 104th Avenue #103
Northglenn, Colo. 80233

This is another organization geared to owners of secretarial service businesses. It is nonprofit and offers a lot
of advice.

8. Interior Design

American Society of Interior Designers
1430 Broadway
New York, N.Y. 10018
(212) 944–9220

Although this professional association does not provide
information on setting up an interior design business, it
does sponsor scholarship competitions for research in the
field and conduct local chapter meetings on specific areas
of interior design. It also publishes a student career guide.

9. Public Relations

The Public Relations Society of America, Inc.
National Headquarters
845 Third Avenue
New York, N.Y. 10022
(212) 826–1750

A professional society for anyone practicing P.R.—as an employee of a P.R. firm, a PR person within a corporation, or as a self-employed P.R. freelancer. PRSA offers members professional development programs and information.

10. Women's Reference Sources

American Business Women's Association
9100 Ward Pkwy.
Kansas City, Mo. 64114

A nonprofit organization with 2,100 local groups, ABWA provides educational programs, support, and advice to any woman who owns or operates her own business.

National Alliance of Home-Based Businesswomen
P.O. Box 95
Norwood, N.J. 07648

A support and educational organization set up to offer financial, management, and organizational advice to any women running a business out of her home. Their book: *Women Working Home* (2nd edition), by Marion Behr and Wendy Lazar, is a valuable compendium of business advice. It is available from P.O. Box 237, Norwood, N.J. 07648, or in bookstores through Rodale Press.

Women Entrepreneurs
2030 Union Street, Suite 310
San Francisco, Calif. 94123

Organized for women business owners, WE offers a wide range of seminars and workshops (some in conjunction with the Small Business Organization) and all kinds of business issues.

American Women's Economic Development Corporation
60 East 42nd Street
New York, N.Y. 10165
(toll free:1-800-222-AWED
NY State: 1-800-442-AWED)

A very strong, helpful organization that offers counseling
and advice to beginning and established businesswomen
through personal counseling sessions or over their toll-
free number (1-800-222-AWED). They charge a nominal
fee for both phone and personal sessions. This is a very
helpful group.

Women's Inter-Art Center
549 West 52nd Street
New York, N.Y. 10019
(212) 246-1050

An active advocate for women artists, WIC offers sponsorship of theater productions, gallery shows, and poetry
readings, plus support for all women in the various arts.

The International Women's Writing Guild
Caller Box 810, Gracie Station
New York, N.Y.
(212) 737-7536

Aspiring and professional women writers are helped in
placing their work with literary agents and are given the
opportunity to work together by this organization.

National Federation of Press Women
Box 99
Blue Springs, Mo. 64015

All full-time and freelance journalists (male and female)
are eligible for membership. The Federation offers educational programs and maintains a speaker's bureau.

Association des Restauratrices Cuisinières
219 Rue Saint-Honoré
F-75001 Paris, France

This association plans to provide apprenticeships and jobs
for women as chefs in a heavily male-dominated field.

U.S. Department of Labor
Women's Bureau
U.S. Dept. of Labor
Washington, D.C. 20210

The Bureau maintains publications relating to working women.

U.S. Department of Commerce
Bureau of the Census
Public Information Office
Washington, D.C. 20233
(202) 763–4040

The Department of Commerce issues a book called *Women-Owned Businesses* that is a complete survey of the status of women entrepreneurs. See section 1, "General Business Advice and Information Resources," on page 131 for additional information.

New England Women Business Owners
4 Brattle Street, Suite 306
Cambridge, Mass. 02138

A network of women in the region who run their own businesses. They provide support and advice.

Women Business Owners of New York
342 Madison Avenue, Rm 514
New York, N.Y. 10173
(212) 370–1865

Although they provide educational seminars on all aspects of business management to women in the N.Y. area, this group does not offer individual counseling. For information about womens business groups in your region of the country check with your local Chamber of Commerce, the National Organization of Women or your State Department of Commerce.

Index

About the Author

Kalia Lulow has been a freelance writer in New York City for the past seven years. During that time she has co-written nine books, including Marjorie Reed's *Entertaining All Year Round*, Dr. Friedman's *Vision Training Program* and *Helena Rubinstein's Book of the Sun*. She also writes for ABC TV Children's Programming.

PLANNING YOUR CAREER
from
BEGINNING TO END...
from
Ballantine Books